So Who's Perfect?

"But we have this treasure in earthen vessels"
(2 Cor. 4:7).

So Who's Perfect?

A Candid Look at Our Humanness

by
Dick Howard

Beacon Hill Press of Kansas City
Kansas City, Missouri

Permission to quote from the following copyrighted versions of the Bible is acknowledged with appreciation:

The *Amplified Old Testament* (Amp.), copyright © 1962, 1964 by Zondervan Publishing House. The *Amplified New Testament,* © 1958 by the Lockman Foundation.

The *New American Standard Bible* (NASB), © The Lockman Foundation, 1960, 1962, 1963, 1968, 1971, 1972, 1973, 1975, 1977.

The *New Testament in Modern English* (Phillips), Revised Edition © J. B. Phillips, 1958, 1960, 1972. By permission of the Macmillan Publishing Co.

The *Revised Standard Version* (RSV), copyrighted 1946, 1952, © 1971, 1973.

Unless otherwise indicated all scripture quotations are taken from the *New American Standard Bible* (NASB).

Dedicated

to those who know me best

To Wini—my devoted wife for more than 40 years

To Judi—my daughter, now serving with her family in
          Swaziland under special missionary appointment

To Roy—my son, an aspiring teacher and writer

Contents

Foreword 9

Preface 11

Prologue 13

PART I—WHAT'S WRONG? 17
    1. How Is It Possible? 19
    2. Hush-Hush! 22
    3. A Must 25

PART II—A BIG DIFFERENCE 29
    4. A Vital Distinction 31
    5. Our Treasure Today 35
    6. Our Vessel Today 42

PART III—MEET A STRANGER 47
    7. We Have Two Sides 49
       Chart 1 52
    8. What We Are—Inner and Outer 53
       Chart 2 55
    9. What Makes Us What We Are? 56
       Chart 3 62
    10. Why Did We Do It? 63
       Chart 4 65
    11. God's Theater of Operations 66

PART IV—WHAT CAN BE DONE? 69

    Chart 5 70

  12. Some Wrong Ideas 71

  13. What About Our Body? 74

  14. Living Under Discipline 78

  15. The Negative Is Never the End 83

PART V—MISUSED DESIRES DISCIPLINED 87

    Chart 6 88

  16. What Is Desire? 89

  17. Temptation or Sin? 91

  18. What Sin Leaves Behind 96

  19. Deliverance from the Old 102

  20. Discovering the New 108

  21. Watch Out! 115

PART VI—IMPULSIVE BEHAVIOR DISCIPLINED 119

    Chart 7 121

  22. Personality Quirks 123

  23. The Big Bugaboo 125

  24. God's Guarantee 128

  25. The Expulsive Power of a New Affection 131

  26. Some Practical Help 133

  27. The Goal Supreme 137

Epilogue 139

Notes 140

Here is a book that is long overdue! It is a candid and helpful look at the human side of living. Many of us have been asking the questions, about our human weaknesses, for a long time. Now, Dick Howard in this volume has given us some answers. Strange, I think, that so much that is written is theoretical, theological, and yes, even threatening—like, "How can I ever wrap my mind and living around that?" Now all of us know that the theological and the technical need to be written. But Dick Howard has done all of us, preachers and laymen, a favor in writing *So Who's Perfect?*

Howard has dared to peel back the veneer and probe at our warts and weaknesses. And the surgery leads to healing! Dick's keen ability to bring the Word and God into man's predicament and problems is what makes the book so valuable. It is scriptural, reasonable, practical, and honest, without being elementary or polemic.

This book has the love and logic of a dedicated minister and educator. One will discover, as he reads this book, that Dick Howard is not writing from some ivory tower. He has walked the common roads of life and experienced the trials, tests, and temptations of which he writes. Dick's academic credentials give the book a balance that makes it both practical and professional.

Some will remember Dick's helpful book on suffering—*Where on Earth Is God?* It had a good acceptance, and I predict the same for *So Who's Perfect?* Dick is writing in the areas where we all live—we're searching, inquiring, and probing. Dick has a word—and a hopeful one it is—that answers questions and puts life in perspective. It gives some handles.

As you read, get ready to say, "Yeah, that's me!" Then,

read on and welcome the wisdom and help that is within
these pages.

C. Neil Strait, *District Superintendent*
Michigan District Church of the Nazarene
Grand Rapids, Michigan

When was the last time you heard it (or maybe said it yourself)—"After all, no one is perfect." Yet, Jesus said, in the Sermon on the Mount: "Therefore you are to be perfect, as your heavenly Father is perfect" (Matt. 5:48). Obviously something is wrong here. Do *you* have problems with Jesus' command? We know our own limitations and weaknesses; we aren't perfect in the way we live.

The confusion is because we are talking about two different things. When we speak of perfection, we mean action or performance—conduct that is without flaw. Everyone knows that only God is perfect in that sense. Is this not what Jesus meant when He told the rich young ruler, "No one is good except God alone" (Luke 18:19)?

But that is not what Jesus was speaking about. His command is the climax of a searching message on how we should treat each other. "You have heard that it was said, 'YOU SHALL LOVE YOUR NEIGHBORS, and hate your enemy.' But I say to you, love your enemies, and pray for those who persecute you" (Matt. 5:43-44). This would make us "sons of [our] Father" (v. 45). In this sense we would be "perfect" like Him—in a relationship of love. Such a relationship is love and prayer from the heart.

We all struggle with our imperfection of conduct—or should. Often we fall short of the standard we know is Christlike. We have the love Jesus spoke about in our hearts, but we don't express it as we should. It is this conflict—between what we have in our hearts and what we express in our lives—that will be examined in the pages that follow.

An early draft of this material was thoroughly critiqued by several friends, and I am deeply indebted to them. Rev. C.

Neil Strait, whose suggestion launched this project, has been a great source of encouragement. Rev. Arthur Fallon, my closest pastoral friend of many years, has given many valuable suggestions. Dr. Lyle Flinner, a professor at Bethany Nazarene College and former teaching colleague of mine, went through the manuscript carefully and offered inestimable assistance, especially with the psychological details. Dr. Timothy L. Smith, taking time out of a busy schedule, spent many hours reading two drafts and gave wise counsel and assistance. Finally, my faithful wife, Wini, read and reread the material—after *hearing* it many times in seminars—correcting errors and suggesting both content and style. For all of this valuable and loving assistance a "thank you" sounds pitifully inadequate.

This book is presented with the earnest prayer that God may graciously use in written form what He has seemingly blessed through the spoken word.

DICK HOWARD
Bethany, Okla.

Prologue

You would have thought I had just confessed to adultery! The dozen or so preachers looked at each other with pained amazement. For once they were speechless. Finally, after what seemed like an eternity, Jim Smith, the patriarch of the group, spoke: "Dick is having problems. Let's gather around the altar and pray with him."

Now, after almost 40 years, the recollection is still painful. My spiritual agony and despair had reached the breaking point. I could stand it no longer. That day, while meeting with several neighboring pastors in an area ministerial meeting, I had suddenly interrupted the planned program with a cry for help. "Why, if our hearts are filled with love, do we do and say unloving things, usually to those we love the most?" For months I had struggled and suffered—alone. But I could not be a hypocrite! I would rather throw in the towel. I had come to the very edge of a spiritual precipice. What countless tests and temptations had failed to do, my soul despair was about to accomplish. I was ready to abandon my faith. This cry for help was my last hope.

Only a few months before, my bride had joined me in the tiny church I was pastoring. With excitement and anticipation we welcomed the challenge of ministering to our first congregation. School, with its abnormal demands, was behind us, and our future together was bright and promising. Our salary was meager, but we were not afraid of sacrifice and hard work. All we wanted was our own home and church.

That beautiful dream had been shattered by a painful nightmare. Again and again irritability and impatience had marred the harmony of our home. There were angry words and unpleasant confrontations. Instead of loving fellowship, there was often the deep hurt of misunderstanding and estrangement. I knew that in great part I was at fault, and my wife was suffering a human hell of disappointment and disillusionment.

I was engulfed by guilt and bewilderment. I understood my theology and knew my heart was filled with God's love—but I didn't always act like it. WHY? I read everything that I could lay my hands on, but could find no help. No one *would* draw the line between human infirmity and sin. Countless hours were spent at the altar of my church—an altar built by my own hands. I pled with God! I begged Him to change me dramatically and miraculously so that my every word and action would reflect His love. But it did not happen! Now, at this zone meeting, with despairing shame I had bared my inner heart for all to see.

After a few sincere and earnest prayers at the altar, my ministerial brothers went their various ways. But I had received help—from an unexpected source! I'll never be able to explain how it happened, but no fewer than three-fourths of my friends managed to share a private word with me before leaving. In substance they all said the same thing. "Don't let that bother you, Dick; we all have the same problem." But they had refused to discuss it in public!

The meeting had been held in the church of my closest pastor friend, and I discovered that Bob was having difficulties, too! We did not feel like eating lunch. Instead we spent the afternoon praying, reading the Bible, and sharing. When dinnertime came, we still weren't hungry and continued our searching late in the evening.

During that afternoon and evening God helped me to see, for the first time, the difference between the "treasure" in my heart and the "vessel" through which it must be seen. That is where the answer to my quest began.

The human personality is very complex. There are no simple explanations for our many conflicts. I am certain that what is to follow is not a complete answer to the entire problem I had. But my darkness and confusion slowly dissolved as I began to understand *myself.* That was the basic difficulty. I hadn't realized the lasting effect of college years. An excessive load of class work had been necessary because of matriculation requirements. At the same time I had been forced to work long hours to meet the expense of a college education in a depression economy. (Government loans were unheard of then!) All of the resulting tension was intensified by a compulsion to strive for academic excellence in preparation for the Christian ministry. God expected my best! I felt well and had no trouble eating or sleeping. Yet all the time this combination of pressures was tightly winding my nerves like a clock spring. When I tried to settle down to a normal life my nerves snapped. They were left jangled and raw. Even minor irritations were aggravated beyond reasonable limits. I was plagued with insomnia, and my doctor told me that I was on the verge of a nervous breakdown.

This was the "vessel" in which my heart "treasure" was housed. Is it any wonder I was having problems?

PART I—WHAT'S WRONG?

Something seems to be wrong! Spiritually minded people everywhere are finding this is their number one question—and problem. How can we put the need to live a holy life together with our humanness? When we are honest we know all about our failures. Is holy living possible while we are *in* the flesh? Is it an impossible dream?

Why isn't this question clearly dealt with in our churches? We don't hear any sermons on the subject. We can hardly find books that treat it. WHY?

Yet it is so important! How can we answer our friends who say a holy life isn't possible here in this world? Are other people as concerned as we are? Can we forget those who we know have left our fellowship because of discouragement over their human failures?

1
How Is It Possible?

How many of us have been struggling with this question: How can I reconcile God's clear call to live a holy life with the painfully obvious fact of my human weakness? When I take a long, honest look at myself, do the two appear to come together about as well as oil and water? Am I struggling to fit the proverbial square peg into a round hole? Yet I must face up to the issue. God expects me to live a holy life. But how is it possible with my limitations, failures, and personality problems? Am I fooling myself?

Admittedly, we in the Wesleyan tradition have a problem. We take seriously the scriptural admonition to live a holy life. It is difficult for us to understand how anyone can miss this insistent emphasis in the Bible. Just as those in the old covenant were named God's *chosen* people, so those in the new covenant are from the beginning called His *holy* ones. That is what "saint" means (KJV), as repeatedly used by Paul. Peter, quoting from the Old Testament, sums up this central message of the Bible: "But like the Holy One who called you, be holy yourselves also . . . because it is written, 'You SHALL BE HOLY, FOR I AM HOLY'" (1 Pet. 1:15-16). He goes on to identify the followers of Christ as "A CHOSEN RACE, a royal PRIESTHOOD, A HOLY NATION, A PEOPLE FOR God's OWN POSSESSION" (2:9). Is this not God's main purpose in redemption? (Cf. Titus 2:14.) Jesus himself voiced the same truth: "Therefore you are to be perfect, as your heavenly Father is perfect" (Matt. 5:48).

Furthermore, holy living means nothing less than total victory over sin. Again and again the standard is raised. This is the theme of the New Testament. When John the Baptist first laid eyes on Jesus, he cried: "Behold, the Lamb of God who takes away the sin of the world" (John 1:29). Paul asked: "How shall we who died to sin still live in it?" (Rom. 6:2). As the first century wound down to a close the aged John wrote: "The blood of Jesus His Son cleanses us from all sin" (1 John 1:7).

While we are persuaded of the truth of this scriptural teaching, we are still faced with the fact of our humanness. This life of victory over sin is to be experienced here and now—*as we live in the flesh.* Can we be holy and still be human? Does not one cancel out the other?

Without doubt our dismay is intensified by the rejection of the Wesleyan doctrine of holiness by a large number of modern evangelicals. They simply conclude it is impossible to live victoriously over sin while we are in the flesh, and for us to claim such is folly and sheer self-deception. From their point of view, to be human is not simply to err—but to sin.

For them the sting that "sinning sainthood" must produce is deadened by the persuasion that our *relationship* with God is not affected by our sin. Some are convinced that our sin is not reckoned (as sin) by God. It is even suggested that God ignores how we live, once we have confessed faith in Christ, and only sees us in Him. That is why a well-known bishop in a liturgical denomination could write: "The only difference between a saint and sinner is that the saint goes to church." However, many more see their sins as rupturing their *fellowship* with God, while their *relationship* with Him (as sons) is not severed. The only type of holiness possible for them is what the theologians call "positional."[1] They are holy in "standing," but not in living.

This is an excellent example of mistaking the branch for the tree. How often it happens when we use the Bible. Positional sanctification is *one* aspect of the New Testament teaching on holiness. Christ Jesus "became to us wisdom from God and righteousness and sanctification and redemption" (1 Cor. 1:30). But, significantly, we have that position only as and because we are part of the family of God. It is a corporate concept. The children of Israel were God's chosen people—but always as a group. So as believers we are God's holy ones—but never as *individual* believers!

Concerning our bodies, the total pessimism so often found in modern evangelical theology is not shared by the New Testament. In fact, the first heretics in the church were branded as such over this very issue. The Gnostics taught that only spirit was good and all matter, including our human bodies, was inherently and forever evil. Such teaching was rejected as a perversion of the faith. To make sin inevitable as long as we live in these mortal bodies identifies us as relatives of those ancient heretics.

Peter was careful to leave no question as to his meaning. A phrase in the above quotation was purposely omitted. "Be holy yourselves also *in all your behavior*" (1 Pet. 1:15, italics added). Clearly this is holiness in *living* and not just in *standing* (cf. Titus 2:11-12). We can't find escape in some relationship that ignores what we are and do. So we are faced with the question: How is it possible for us to live a holy life with all of our limitations, weaknesses, failures, and personality problems? The answer to that question is our quest.

2
Hush-Hush!

Unfortunately, the subject of holy living and human infirmity is seldom dealt with in Wesleyan circles, from pulpit or pen. We don't talk much about it—out in the open. Perhaps to do so would seem like washing our dirty linen in public. Few books have been written specifically on the subject. Those that are written too often skirt the central issues, and generalizations leave the reader confused and bewildered. A clear line is not drawn between sin and human failures. Many pulpits resound with the full range of biblical truth, including messages on holy living. But a sermon relating such living to our human limitations is a rarity. Many of us facing the problem struggle with it alone.

Why the hush-hush? Could it be, in part, that we preachers fear misunderstanding? Let there be no question, this is one of the easiest places in the world to be misunderstood! It is often thought that a discussion of human weakness gives people excuses for unholy living. None who preach enjoy being on that spot, but that is virtually an occupational hazard for an effective preacher. When we realize how many are deeply hurting over this question, where is a better cause for which to be a martyr?

Another possible reason for the neglect is that most preachers like to be dogmatic. We feel more at ease when we can herald our good news with a ring of certainty. "This is the way it is!" But we dare not dogmatize here. To do so in this arena only unmasks our own perplexity and struggle. Often a preacher's confident assertions are voiced to convince himself more than his hearers.

Certainly a major reason that more is not said about human weakness is that it is not explicitly examined in the New Testament. A large part of our difficulty is that human failures, limitations, and so on are not dealt with by name. If they were, we would not be so perplexed. These omissions should not come as a surprise, however. Many of our personal problems today are not discussed in Scripture. We are not specifically advised about how to handle such practical matters as shattering sickness, unnerving fears, tensions in the home, family conflicts, frustrations at work, or economic pressures. The Bible never mentions by name the modern moral issues of drug abuse, abortion, racial discrimination, and environmental pollution.

It is no wonder that the New Testament does not deal with such particular needs. Much of it, especially Paul's letters, was written in the heat of missionary evangelism. Even more significantly, the pervading atmosphere of the New Testament is the immediate return of Christ. In fact, He was due yesterday! Even when Paul paused to deal with some intensely practical problems in the Corinthian church, his overriding concern was that they maintain the status quo— because "the time has been shortened" (1 Cor. 7:29). This has triggered a barrage of unjust criticism of Paul. Unless we understand Paul's perspective, his counsel is alien to the basic principles of justice. A failure to catch the inherent nature of biblical revelation has resulted in finding the New Testament guilty of insensitivity to such a grave issue as human slavery.

But does this mean there is no help for us in God's Word? Perish the thought! Although the Scriptures do not *explicitly* consider holiness and human frailty, we shall find *implicit principles* through which the Lord can minister to us. We shall try to project answers to our questions on the basis of the principles that are clearly given. Actually, this is the correct way to use the Bible, whatever our need. The Bible does not contain a magical "how to," custom-fitted to our every situation; nor is it a list of laws and rules governing our conduct in detail. Instead, it is God's message to us. We must receive that message and then apply it to our specific circumstances. It is here that the Holy Spirit fills the role promised by Jesus (cf. John 14:26). Under His loving tutelage, the truth of God's Word becomes personally meaningful to us.

We could well be rushing in "where angels fear to tread," but we must face honestly and openly the facts of which most of us are painfully aware.

3
A Must

Do we have an option? Must not the problem before us be honestly admitted and discussed? Ignoring it will not eradicate it. When we open our eyes, it is still there. But the fact that the problem simply will not go away is by no means the only, or most important, reason to consider the matter. There are more urgent reasons why we must probe this puzzle of how our humanness can be reconciled with God's requirement for holy living.

It is necessary to face candidly the facts if we expect those who disagree with us theologically to take us seriously. Many point to human imperfections as proof positive that there is no such thing as living a holy life. They say that to profess it is self-deception, if not hypocrisy. Without a doubt much of the discrediting of the holiness message is based on misconceptions. But from where do these mistaken ideas come? Of course, there will always be those in every theological camp who delight in building straw men and then triumphantly demolishing them. More often, however, the basic problem is a lack of communication and the misunderstanding it brings. If we are unwilling or unable to discuss how holy living is related to human weakness, we have no answer to their disclaimers. This does not mean that we have gone on the defensive, but rather that we want our message understood.

Far more important than the stated reasons is the near tragic result among many of our *own* people if we don't face and then deal with this troublesome question. How are holy living and human frailty to be reconciled? There are always those of us who fail to see the problem—especially in ourselves. We are blind to that which is glaringly visible to others. Unfortunately, we are often the last ones to realize our own failures. As a result, many of us live on a far too superficial spiritual plane and never come to grips with our imperfections.

But many of us *do* see our shortcomings. Yet we are left to battle them alone. Because nothing is publicly said about this common spiritual struggle, it is easy for us to conclude that we are the only ones with such a problem. It never occurs to us that someone else, perhaps a friend, is facing a similar kind of conflict. When we have no encouragement to share our mutual needs openly, we can create a climate of guilt in which admission of need automatically produces condemnation. This is not a matter of misery loving company. Rather, it is a source of encouragement to know that we aren't the only ones with such distress. There are sad, even tragic, accounts of those who have struggled and suffered alone with their personal failures for many years.

Others of us recognize that we do not measure up to the standard of holy living as we understand it. We accept the truth of the holy life rationally. We know the Bible teaches it. Yet there are conditions in our lives that appear to make such a life unattainable. Perhaps it is tension in our home or a conflict at work or any of a score of such things. When the problem of human frailties is not dealt with openly and honestly, it is understandable why we can conclude: "In my situation holy living is impossible!" We need to realize what a horrible indictment such a conclusion fabricates against God. What kind of a tyrant would God be if He required of us that which is impossible? Yet it would be shocking to most of us if we knew how many there are in our church fellowship who have come to this conclusion.

Undoubtedly the most heartbreaking consequence of not openly dealing with the question of holy living and human frailty is the casualty list. Only God knows the countless number of us who have become discouraged, defeated, and eventually destroyed spiritually because of failures in this vital area. We know the sincerity of our hearts! We honestly tried to obey as best we knew. There was nothing that we were unwilling to do, and our consecration was without reservation. Yet it simply didn't work for us, at least as the experience of holiness had been presented to us.

We must candidly admit that we fall far short of the standard that has been set before us. If we were to go to the altar a dozen times, there would be nothing more we could do or give. So many have turned away or dropped by the wayside as spiritual casualties. I have come to believe very strongly that this produces more spiritual fatalities *than all other causes combined.* Of course, few of us will admit it. We lay down a smoke screen of excuses and justifications for our failure. But when the truth is fully known, our biggest disappointment is with *ourselves.*

There is too much at stake to quietly sweep under the carpet the painful fact of human failures among holiness people. It can and must be reconciled with God's call to a holy life.

PART II—A BIG DIFFERENCE

Now that we are looking at the problem, where do we start to find answers? The beginning place is with ourselves. The New Testament (indeed the whole Bible) has a very clear understanding of us as human persons. This understanding is based on a simple observation or experiencing of ourselves.

There is a big difference between what we are inside (in our hearts) and what we are outside (in our living). Paul described this difference as the "treasure" (within) and the "vessel" (without). This vital distinction must become clear to us. That is where we begin.

4
A Vital Distinction

When writing to the Corinthians, Paul made a vital distinction that provides a key to finding the pieces of the puzzle we have been examining: How can human failure be reconciled with holy living? He said: "But we have this treasure in earthen vessels" (2 Cor. 4:7). There is a crucial difference between our treasure and the vessel in which it is housed!

What is the "treasure" Paul spoke about? We don't want to be guilty of tearing a phrase out of its context and using it simply for our purposes. The treasure is the gospel of the new covenant that Paul had ministered to the Corinthians.

To understand what he meant we must see Paul's graphic contrast. It was a shocking assertion for a Jew to make. He vividly compared his ministry with that of Moses. That simply was not done! He said that the old covenant, given to Moses on Mount Sinai, was written "in letters engraved on stones" (2 Cor. 3:7). It had come with such glory that Moses descended from the holy mountain with his face veiled, lest the people see God's glory and perish (vv. 7, 13; cf. Exod. 34:33-35). But that glory was "fading"—literally "being done away" (*katargoumēn*, 2 Cor. 3:7, 11, 13). The old covenant had become a "ministry of condemnation . . . [and] death" (vv. 9, 7) because "the letter kills" (v. 6; cf. Rom. 7:6). Incredibly, Paul concluded that in comparison with the glory revealed in Christ, *Mount Sinai had no glory* (2 Cor. 3:10). He recognized that such speech was indeed bold, but his living hope in Christ demanded it (v. 12).

Using this imagery, Paul pictured the Jews of his day as still veiled when the old covenant was read. But now the veil was on their hearts, and their minds were darkened (vv. 14-15). Apparently Paul was alluding to this darkness surrounding the old covenant and what is associated with it, when he caustically denied "peddling" (2:17, margin, "corrupting") or "adulterating" (4:2) the Word of God.

In stark contrast to Moses, Paul proclaimed an "unveiled" gospel: "But whenever a man turns to the Lord, the veil is taken away" (3:16). Instead of the enslaving letter of the old covenant, which kills, the freedom of the new covenant of the Spirit brought life (v. 6). Specifically, it was the glorious vision of "the light of the knowledge of the glory of God in the face of Christ" (4:6). "But we all, with unveiled face beholding as in a mirror the glory of the Lord, are being transformed[1] into the same image from glory to glory, just as from the Lord, the Spirit" (3:18).

Continuing the same figure, Paul viewed the unbelievers, to whom he was attempting to minister, as victims of the mind-blinding work of Satan (4:4). The glorious light of the gospel was veiled so that the "unseeing" unbelievers were perishing instead of discovering life.

This is the treasure—the whole life-giving gospel of the glory of God. "But we have this treasure in earthen vessels" (4:7).

What does Paul mean by the "earthen vessels"? Quite obviously they are the body or "mortal flesh" (vv. 10-11). But he was speaking of far more than the *physical* body, as his own testimony makes plain (cf. vv. 8-9). We might call it the human "house." In fact, Paul used that very term (*oikia,* 5:1) as well as "tent" or "tabernacle" (*skēnous,* vv. 1, 4). By this he meant the *whole* outer "man" (*anthrōpos,* 4:16). In more modern terms it comprises the physical and the psychological being, often called "psychosomatic," the "whole person."

Furthermore, this body is an "earthen" vessel. To portray it, Paul used a vivid Greek word *(ostrakinos)* often found in pre-Christian literature. Its literal meaning is "earthenware," and it was specifically related to fragile or kiln-baked pottery. At times it even described the brittle covering of a shellfish. It is clearly a picture of fragility or breakableness. Similarly, the human house is fragile, weak, and breakable.

In the immediate context Paul contrasted this fragile outer man (body) with the inner man. While the outer is decaying, the inner is being daily renewed (2 Cor. 4:16). We are urged to focus our attention on the unseen (inner man) because it is eternal. That which is seen (outer man) is temporal (v. 18). The climaxing contrast is between the present and future outer man, wherein lies the believer's blessed hope. When our "earthly tent . . . is torn down," we have a new "house" already prepared for us. It is "a house not made with hands, eternal in the heavens" (5:1).

Paul is very careful to distinguish the Christian's hope from current Greek expectations of immortality in some future life without a body. The man of faith does not desire to be "unclothed," but rather to be *further* clothed, lest he be found naked (2 Cor. 5:3-4). He will not *escape* from his body but instead will *exchange* it for a body of glory (cf. 1 Cor. 15:42-44). That which is mortal will be "swallowed up by life" (2 Cor. 5:4).

In spite of every imaginable form of physical and psychological persecution Paul was being sustained. His fragile human house was preserved by God (4:8-9). Paul viewed this as a miracle. He goes on to describe how he was *literally* facing death and destruction every day and thus was *figuratively* entering into Jesus' death. His deliverance showed forth the resurrection of Jesus. The very same power that raised Jesus from the grave was keeping Paul alive. His Lord was being "manifested"—vividly portrayed—in his human house in spite of his weaknesses (vv. 10-12).

Most New Testament scholars place Paul in Ephesus near the time that he wrote the second Corinthian letter. His description of suffering and persecution most likely relates to his experiences briefly described in Acts 19:23-41. In a passing reference he spoke of fighting with wild beasts at Ephesus (1 Cor. 15:32). He gave a more graphic and personal account in the introduction of a later letter.

> For just as the sufferings of Christ are ours in abundance, so also our comfort is abundant through Christ. But if we are afflicted, it is for your comfort and salvation; or if we are comforted, it is for your comfort, which is effective in the patient enduring of the same sufferings which we also suffer; and our hope for you is firmly grounded, knowing that as you are sharers of our sufferings, so also you are sharers of our comfort. For we do not want you to be unaware, brethren, of our affliction which came to us in Asia, that we were burdened excessively, beyond our strength, so that we despaired even of life; indeed, we had the sentence of death within ourselves in order that we should not trust in ourselves, but in God who raises the dead; who delivered us from so great a peril of death, and will deliver us, He on whom we have set our hope. And He will yet deliver us (2 Cor. 1:5-10).

Of greatest importance to our study, then, is Paul's vital distinction between the inner and outer man. In his case, the limitations and fragilities of the outer man were revealed through his tests and trials. For us the "earthiness" of our outer man is discovered in a myriad of experiences. Yet the same distinction exists. We must learn to know the difference between the "treasure" and the "vessel."

5

Our Treasure Today

Thank God we can possess the treasure today! It is still the "whole life-giving gospel of the glory of God." But exactly of what does that consist? To answer that question adequately would take several volumes of biblical theology. Although a thorough review of our blessings in Christ would be spiritually profitable, such is not our objective. We can only set forth the heart of it.[1]

The gospel of good news, of our Lord Jesus Christ, begins with the promise of a wondrous new *relationship* with God. As sinners—and all of us were sinners (Rom. 3:23)—we stood under the judgment of God, with its wrath and condemnation. "So then as through one transgression there resulted condemnation to all men" (Rom. 5:18). But through faith in the Cross, God's love gift to all men, our status with God is dramatically altered and veritably revolutionized. Paul used several vivid word pictures to describe this incredible truth.

Using the metaphor of the slave market, he portrayed the Cross as *redeeming* or ransoming all men from sin's slavery (Rom. 3:24). Peter graphically described the same wonder.

> Knowing that you were not redeemed with perishable things like silver or gold from your futile way of life inherited from your forefathers, but with precious blood,

as of a lamb unblemished and spotless, the blood of
Christ *(1 Pet. 1:18-19).*

Every sinner is purchased out of slavery by the Cross. With a
different figure Paul spoke of the *reconciliation* provided for
all who are alienated from God by their sins (cf. Eph. 2:
12-19). It was God who reconciled us unto himself.

But that universal *provision* of the Cross must become
our own personal *possession.* How can such an unbelievable
thing occur? The glorious message of the gospel is this: Faith
makes it happen! In using the imagery of the law court, Paul
depicted it as *justification* (Rom. 3:24). This does not mean
acquittal, because that signifies innocence, and *we are guilty!*
Standing before the Judge of all the earth, as we have faith in
the cross death of Christ for us, God pronounces us free. All
charges are canceled. Before Him we now stand justified and
lovingly accepted.

"Justification by faith" became the battle cry of the Protestant Reformation and is widely thought to be basic to Pauline theology. Yet surprisingly he used the idea only when he
was extensively combating his Judaistic opponents, namely
in Romans and Galatians. The Judaizers were Christian Jews
who had merely added faith in Jesus Christ as Messiah to
their Jewish religion. They remained convinced that one had
to be a Jew in order to attain salvation. When they sought to
impose the Mosaic law on his Gentile converts, Paul developed the doctrine of justification by faith. Our legal acceptance by God was not by the works of the law but by grace
through faith (cf. Gal. 2:16).

Paul declared the same truth in his other letters with a
concept more familiar to us. When we make the glorious provision of the Cross our own personal possession by faith—
we are *forgiven:* "For He delivered us from the domain of
darkness, and transferred us to the kingdom of His beloved
Son, in whom we have redemption, the forgiveness of sins"
(Col. 1:13-14).

We can more readily understand this idea. We know by experience how forgiveness heals ruptured human relationships. In a more complete sense, our alienation and separation from God comes to an end as He lovingly forgives all our sins and treats us as if we had never been away.

With still another metaphor Paul described our new relationship with God through faith. "You have received a spirit of adoption as sons by which we cry out, 'Abba! Father!'" (Rom. 8:15). Incredibly, as forgiven sinners we become part of His family—with all that *adoption* meant in first-century culture and customs. Old family ties and associations are canceled—just as if they had never existed. Debts are erased, relationships are severed, past failures are forgotten, hopelessness and despair are taken away. We are now members of a new family, God's family. Beyond belief, all that is His now belongs to us! "And if children, heirs also, heirs of God and fellow heirs with Christ" (Rom. 8:17). It is almost more than our finite minds can grasp.

As members of God's family we are *holy.* Everything that belongs to Him is holy—the Temple (even the pots and pans!), the land (Palestine), the city (Jerusalem), and so on. So we, too, are holy. It is little wonder that the favorite name for the earliest followers of Christ was "holy ones" ("saints" in the KJV). However, it must always be remembered that we are thus *positionally* holy—in theological terms—only as we are part of the family of God.

In our new family there is *fellowship* previously undreamed of. "God is faithful, through whom you were called into fellowship with His Son, Jesus Christ our Lord" (1 Cor. 1:9). This fellowship brings peace and joy to our sin-troubled hearts. "Therefore having been justified by faith, we have peace with God through our Lord Jesus Christ, . . . and we exult [rejoice] in hope of the glory of God" (Rom. 5:1-3).

Perhaps the greatest privilege of all is *access (prosagōgē).* "Through him we have obtained access to this grace in which we stand" (Rom. 5:2, RSV). For us today it is very difficult to even vaguely appreciate what this meant to the earliest believers. For the Jew, God was awesomely, even frighteningly, "untouchable." Only the high priest, and he only on the Day of Atonement, could enter into the presence of God (in the holy of holies). This was only with great fear and trembling. But now, since Christ "tore in two" the veil of the Temple, from top to bottom (Mark 15:38), there is an open door into God's presence. We so easily forget today that we have our privilege of access to God only at great cost. But thank God, we can now come to Him any time, anywhere, with any need.

As wondrous as this new relationship with God is, the half has not yet been told. Our new outward status *with* God is only one aspect of the gracious possession we have in Christ. At the same time we also possess *a wondrous new subjective experience of God.* Yet there have always been those, from Paul's day until ours, who fail to see anything more in salvation than a new "standing" with God. After Paul had vividly written about the believer's new gracious standing before God (cf. Rom 3:21—5:21), he found it necessary to answer the challenge that the gospel was limited to this. Romans 6—8 strongly emphasizes that our faith not only reconciles us *with* God, but it also brings us into Christ. Repeatedly this is stated by Paul: "Therefore if any man is in Christ, he is a new creature" (2 Cor. 5:17). We become new *persons!* This speaks of the dramatic change *within us.* In Christ we have new life, His life. "He who has the Son has the life; he who does not have the Son of God does not have the life" (1 John 5:12). This is what Jesus spoke about to Nicodemus—being "born again." The technical theological term is "regeneration," which means making alive that which is dead. "Even when we were dead in our transgressions, [God] made us alive together with Christ (by grace you have been saved)" (Eph. 2:5).

But this new life is not mere existence, it is *living*. We are not only alive, but we live a new life in a new way. This is possible because in Christ we are *free* persons as well as *new* persons. As sinners we were enslaved, but in Christ we are set free. Using the imagery of an emancipated slave, Paul pictured the man in Christ as freed from sin (cf. Rom. 6:18, 22). Deliverance from the power of sin makes possible a new life of righteousness. Paul always made it clear that the believer's new life was the *work of God* and not man. "For we are His workmanship, created in Christ Jesus for good works, which God prepared beforehand, that we should walk in them" (Eph. 2:10). As Jesus told Nicodemus, we not only must be born again (from above), but we need to be *born of the Spirit* (cf. John 3:5-6). It is the Holy Spirit who makes our new life possible. It is a life of *certainty*, by faith, and *concern* through love.

One of the essential facts about life is growth. In fact, if we don't grow we won't live very long! The new life we find in Christ *must* grow and develop. When we are born again we begin a journey of spiritual growth. The nature of that growth is clearly described for us. "But grow in the grace and knowledge of our Lord and Savior Jesus Christ" (2 Pet. 3:18). And our spiritual development has a well defined end in view.

> But we all, with unveiled face beholding as in a mirror the glory of the Lord, are being transformed into the same image from glory to glory, just as from the Lord, the Spirit *(2 Cor. 3:18)*.

> For whom He foreknew, He also predestined to become conformed to the image of His Son, that He might be the first-born among many brethren *(Rom. 8:29)*.

How simple and yet so amazing—to be like Christ! We know that such an incredible goal is only possible in the power of the Holy Spirit.

As Wesleyans we believe there is a point on this pilgrimage when a crucial experience takes place that we call "entire sanctification." When we take the new life God has given us and *return* it to Him, Jesus becomes the Lord of our new life. What happens when this takes place? We are totally delivered from the original sin with which we were born and which remained in our lives after we were saved. This "original" sin is understood by some as a perverted relationship with God that can be called "self-sovereignty"[2] and will be described in more detail later (cf. chap. 9). "Sovereignty" means the power of control. In the crisis of entire sanctification this perverted relationship with God—in which man has taken control of his life—*is totally remedied.* Thus entire sanctification does not imply that our spiritual journey has been completed. Instead, it means that the perverted relationship is *entirely* corrected. Then, and only then, can Jesus be truly Lord of our lives.

When this "crisis of control" occurs, one of the greatest miracles possible takes place. *His Spirit and our spirit become one spirit!* Paul spoke of this in a most unlikely place, where he is warning the Corinthian believers about the fatality of consorting with harlots. "But the one who joins himself to the Lord is one spirit with Him" (1 Cor. 6:17). Now we can begin to experience the fuller life of holiness by and through the Spirit. With Jesus as Lord, and self-lordship banished, we discover His strength and power. Paul called this "walking" (cf. Gal. 5:16) and even "marching" (cf. v. 25) by the Spirit in a "continuing companionship" with Him. The result is growth—in understanding, establishment, improved performance, and Christlikeness. Paul summed it all up as "increasing" and "abounding" in love (cf. 1 Thess. 3:12). We increasingly learn that *our work* is to open our lives more widely to Him so He can "will and . . . work [in us] for His good pleasure" (Phil. 2:13). The Greek word for God's work is *energeō,* which is transliterated today as *energize.* God would energize our lives by His Spirit! Thus life by the Spirit is victorious living—victory over sin, because of a new obsession; victory over death, because of a new hope; victory over weakness, because of a new strength; victory over adversity, because of a new security (cf. Romans 8).

Briefly described, this is our treasure today. But we have it in earthen vessels.

6
Our Vessel Today

Stuart Hamblen's song "This Old House" was a top hit in seven different countries at the same time. Yet, as the author related several years later, few ever understood the basic message of the song. The inspiration for the lyrics came from Hamblen's discovery of an old dead prospector, guarded by his half-dead dog, in a deserted and broken-down cabin in the high Sierras—broken windowpanes, shabby curtains, and all. But the writer's purpose was not simply to compose a tearjerker. He recognized in that worn-out cabin a picture of our human house. These mortal bodies also wear out. But, thank God, there is coming a day when we will need them no longer as we go to "meet the saints."

Our concern here is to recognize and remember that this is true of our vessel today. Its limitations and weaknesses are seen in many ways. Sometimes, even as Paul described (2 Cor. 4:8-9), the fragility of our human house is discovered as we go through the storms of life. To be sure, for most of us our tests and trials are not comparable to those with which Paul grappled. Yet we must not forget that multitudes *do* contend with persecution and pressure that threaten their very existence. It is difficult for us, living in peace and prosperity, to comprehend what they face. Little is known, except by those who experience it, what life is *really* like behind the infamous iron and bamboo curtains—particularly for those who resist these oppressive regimes. In recent years worldwide terrorism has added another ghastly dimension to human suffering.

An unofficially "adopted" son and daughter of mine, with their two small children, have known the menace of terrorism for several years of their young lives. Serving as missionaries in one of the strife-torn nations of Africa, Tom and Jane never knew at what hour of the day or night their home could be invaded by half-crazed revolutionaries. A missionary friend living nearby was murdered on his front porch. That at least approaches the testings Paul described!

But we don't have to leave our own land to find people living under intense pressure of many kinds. Poverty, unemployment, ugly discrimination, and a score more social evils—often right in our own neighborhood—cause increasing numbers severe distress and despair.

Yet for most of us, our tests and trials do not involve violence or extreme deprivation. Nevertheless they are very real. Sometimes it is misunderstanding and unfair criticism. It might be acute problems at work or in the home, or even a conflict with our children or in our marriage. Suddenly an accident or sickness occurs, and we have a major crisis on our hands. For many of us, just providing the basic necessities of life takes all of our strength and energy, and we live in a state of constant exhaustion. The list could go on endlessly.[1]

Thank God, He promises and provides all of us with sufficient strength. Many times we don't understand how, but He does it! We make it somehow. We can and must be conquerors by His grace.

Still, the tests and trials of life *do* reveal our human limitations and weaknesses—just as they did for Paul. At such times we, too, are convinced that only God's power enables us to survive. Our human house would be crushed and utterly destroyed without His help. We must honestly recognize that our spiritual treasure exists in a fragile vessel.

The fragility of our human house can be revealed in other ways that Paul did not specify. One method that many of us don't like to consider is our age. At least for several years most of us are sensitive, if not secretive, about how old we are. Yet a very strange change often takes place. As years go by, a surprising number of aging persons increasingly talk about their age with a sense of pride or accomplishment. Have you ever seen this happen? My wife's mother was so secretive about her age that Wini was probably in her teens before she knew how old her mother was. Yet in the last decade of her life, Mother wanted everyone she met to know when she had passed another milestone. Her 95th birthday was a very special occasion.

Yet growing old is one of the most obvious facts of life. Biologists tell us that we hardly begin to live before we start to die. Isn't that inspiring? When we are young, we manage to produce more life cells than we lose. Then we reach a place when the score is about even. Inevitably the days come when we lose more than we gain, and we know what finally happens. We don't like to think about growing old until we remember the alternative. Then it doesn't hurt quite so much.

But advanced years unveil, for all to see, our human infirmities. Few escape the serious limitation, if not total loss, of some physical abilities. Eyesight fails, hearing loss occurs, limbs are crippled with arthritis, brittle bones are broken, and disease wastes our strength. It is simply the human house wearing out!

Even more painful is the deterioration of psychological faculties. Such things as failing memory (although one doesn't need to be very old for this to happen!), lessening understanding, lack of judgment, unreasonable demands, loss of patience, and harsh words so often accompany aging. Some of the saddest experiences I had as a pastor was seeking to minister to young couples who had the trying responsibility of caring for aging parents. They did not understand how Mom or Dad could change so radically. A parent whom they remembered from childhood as being the very essence of patience and understanding, now was totally distraught with the grandchildren. It *is* perplexing! Repeatedly I tried to explain that the *real* person had not changed. Only the house was wearing out.

Our biggest difficulty, however, is not with tests and trials, or even the strain of advanced age. Those who are spiritually sensitive and deeply sincere find their greatest struggle and battle is with *personality failures*—at all ages. Here our limitations, weaknesses, and infirmities are vividly seen, oftentimes to our distress and even despair. It can be any of a score of personality or temperament problems. No two of us have quite the same failures—*but we all do have them.*

It is true that *some* of our difficulty can be traced to years in sin. When we live long years with little thought or consideration for others and have the great obsession of satisfying our own desires, it does put a stamp on our personality. Sin inevitably leaves its mark! When we abuse our natural emotions and desires, we are left to struggle with them in later years. Distinct habit patterns of behavior are developed as we seek to satisfy a sinful heart. Then, after we are converted, we discover that our impulsive actions follow these patterns. We involuntarily react in ways that we formerly did. That is one prime reason why it is so important to be saved when we are young.

Yet a hangover from years in sin hardly explains *all* of our personality flaws. There are deeper reasons that we don't understand. We are left bewildered and distressed by our own actions. Why do we act in ways that we know are not Christlike? Even more disheartening is our sense of helplessness. We can't seem to do anything about it. Repeatedly we plead with God to change us and to make us different. We genuinely don't want to act that way. Still, nothing seems to happen and our personality problems persist.

Paul wrote of being afflicted with a thorn in the flesh (2 Cor. 12:7). Although scholars through the ages have speculated as to what this thorn might be, no one knows with certainty. It is my opinion that Paul struggled with personality failure—perhaps several. Certainly it was hardly possible for a Pharisee—and Paul was raised one—to avoid having some! Furthermore, his letters bear indications that he had problems. The Judaizers, Christian Jews who believed that it was necessary for a Christian to become a Jew, sought to impose the Jewish Law on Paul's Gentile converts in Galatia. In his impassioned letter to these converts, the Apostle condemned his opponents with what appears at times to be intemperate and even crude language—at least by today's standards (cf. Gal. 5:12). Again, Paul's public rebuke of Peter, calling him a hypocrite before the church at Antioch, reflects more than simply a strong or forceful personality (2:11 ff.). When Paul parted company with Barnabas rather than allowing Mark to accompany them on their second missionary journey, his conflict with Barnabas is described as a "sharp disagreement" (Acts 15:39). (To be fair to Paul, it must be noted that his attitude toward Mark beautifully mellowed. One of his last instructions to Timothy was a request for him to bring Mark to see him in prison because "he is useful to me for service" [2 Tim. 4:11].) It is very possible that Paul struggled with a problem of angry impatience a good part of his early Christian life.

Most, if not all, of us *do* have to battle with personality failures of many kinds. It is a very real part of our spiritual lives. What is of utmost importance is to learn—in ourselves and others—to distinguish between the "treasure" and the "vessel." Today our treasure is in earthen vessels that are weak and fragile.

PART III—MEET A STRANGER

After several years of extensive ministry as a pastor, teacher, and evangelist, I am firmly persuaded that many, probably a majority, of our spiritual problems come from a failure to *understand ourselves.* This is particularly so with regard to holy living. We simply are unable to distinguish between the "treasure" and the "vessel," our newness of life and the human house in which it dwells.

As Jesus neared the Cross, He selected three disciples—Peter, James, and John—and gave to them undoubtedly the greatest privilege man has ever known. Taking them into the inner Garden of Gethsemane, He asked them to pray with Him in His darkest hour: "My soul is deeply grieved to the point of death; remain here and keep watch" (Mark 14:34). We all know what happened! As Jesus, in deep soul agony, was taking on himself the sin of the whole world, *they fell asleep.* Not just once, but three times! Yet what was the Master's reaction? In love, but certainly with sadness, He declared: "The spirit is willing, but the flesh is weak" (v. 38). Our Lord knew the difference between the treasure and the vessel.

If we are going to understand this distinction, we must carefully examine the New Testament and determine what it has to say about us as persons. We most likely will meet a stranger. Surprisingly, we discover that neither Paul nor the rest of the New Testament *theoretically* analyzes man or philosophizes about his nature as such.[1] Certainly we cannot bring to the New Testament modern psychology as a science. Those who wrote the Scriptures, under the inspiration of the Holy Spirit, were common and ordinary people with little or no formal education. In fact, most of the New Testament was written through an amanuensis (secretary), because very few in that day could read and even fewer could write. If the New Testament had been put into theoretical or technical terms, people simply would not have understood it. Instead, the Bible is *basically experiential,* and its words, ideas, and concepts are understood as they are mirrored in our experience. When this is forgotten today, confusion results.

7
We Have Two Sides

As we examine the New Testament, we see an obvious distinction and observation about ourselves that we can readily understand experientially. We are a single person with two sides or parts. Although it is not often stated as such, we all are an *inner* man and an *outer* man. Repeatedly the New Testament refers to "man" *(anthrōpos)*, but this is not representative of male in contrast to female. It instead means "person" in the generic sense. Although the biblical language is "man," for the sake of clarity the term "self" will be used.[1]

> Therefore we do not lose heart, but though our outer man is decaying, yet our inner man is being renewed day by day *(2 Cor. 4:16)*.

> That He would grant you . . . to be strengthened with power through His Spirit in the inner man *(Eph. 3: 16)*.

Sometimes Paul expressed the same distinction by "hidden" or "secret" *(kruptos)* in contrast to "visible" or "seen" *(phanerōs)* (cf. Rom. 2:28-29, lit. Gk.).

This view of persons is basic to Jewish thought. When God found it necessary to replace Saul, the first king of Israel, He sent the prophet Samuel to the house of Jesse to anoint the new king. After Jesse had presented his seven stalwart sons, the prophet was certain that none of them was God's choice and asked: "Are these all the children?" Jesse replied:

"There remains yet the youngest, and behold, he is tending the sheep" (1 Sam. 16:11). This is the context for one of the most memorable verses in the Old Testament: "For God sees not as man sees, for man looks at the outward appearance, but the Lord looks at the heart" (v. 7). Here is the vital distinction between *outward* appearance and the *inner* heart.

In the New Testament, the inner self is most often called the "heart" *(kardia)* or the "mind" *(nous).* [2] It is very interesting and important that the New Testament does not basically refer to the *inner self* as the soul! The contrast with which we are so familiar, soul vs. body, is a Greek idea and is not biblical.[3] Instead, the soul has the larger meaning of person or the total self. What about "spirit" *(pneuma)?* Significantly, the Synoptics and Acts use this term to depict the inner self, but Paul has a unique use of the word. The "spirit" is where God and man meet; and when he refers to "spirit," there are always overtones of "Spirit," that is, the Holy Spirit, and vice versa. (In the earliest manuscripts every letter was capitalized.) This is the reason modern English versions have so many variations in their translations of *pneuma.* [4]

The outer self is called the "body" *(sōma)* or the "flesh" *(sarx)* and a few times "our members." We *must* grasp this basic distinction if we ever hope to understand ourselves in the light of the Bible.

What complicates the matter is that all of Western civilization, which includes us, has been extensively influenced by Greek thought. The Greeks made a distinction that sounds similar but is vastly different. Actually, the Greeks looked at a person as *two persons.* There was the soul that was spiritual, intrinsically and entirely good, in reality a "chip" off God, and consequently immortal. In contrast, the body was the direct opposite, being material, hopelessly and helplessly evil, and mortal. There was no possible good in the body. Instead, it was a prison house from which the soul must escape and return to God, often in some form of pantheism, where it became a part of God. Most significant, in direct contradiction to biblical thought, the two (soul and body) could and did exist separately, with the soul in some type of disembodied state.

Unfortunately, these basic Greek ideas greatly influenced the formulation of Christian theology because *every* significant Christian thinker after apostolic times was a Greek or non-Jew! It is understandable why the early Christians used non-Semitic concepts as they sought to communicate with their Greek world. But to bring such an understanding to the Bible, which was written exclusively by Jews,[5] can only cause confusion and misunderstanding. In Jewish thought there can be no whole person without *both* the inner and outer self. That is why we will one day get a new outer self, a resurrected body. When we are through with this earthly physical and psychological body, we are going to receive a new body! We can't be a person without both—an inner and outer self.

So as we try to understand ourselves, we need to keep clear the concept of these "two sides." Mistakenly, some modern evangelicals have been greatly influenced by the Greek view of the outer self. They teach that the body is hopelessly evil and that while we are living in it, sinning is unavoidable. This is actually a revival of Gnosticism, the first heresy that the Christian Church faced. It is "neo-Gnosticism." Most important, *it is not true to the New Testament!*

Let us examine more closely the inner and outer self. To my knowledge the New Testament doesn't explicitly do this but simply recognizes the distinction. In order to understand ourselves, however, we must take a careful look at the distinction.

INNER SELF: HEART, MIND

TAKE TO HEAVEN

OUTER SELF: BODY, FLESH

(LEAVE ON EARTH)

8
What We Are—Inner and Outer

The Bible makes a very simple *experiential* distinction. The inner self is all that one day we are going to take to heaven. In contrast, the outer self is all that one day we will leave behind on earth. We no longer will need the old outer body to express our inner self because we will have a new body.

As seen on Chart 1, the inner heart or mind is our inner personhood. The term *personhood,* as distinct from outer *personality,* is arbitrarily used to describe the inner qualities of character, convictions, and ideals. These are hidden and unseen by other people. Notice that they can be either good or bad (an evil heart or mind was incomprehensible to a Greek). This inner self is revealed or discovered in our attitudes toward God, other people, and our own self.

The outer self, our body or flesh, is the "human house" that is the means or avenue of expression or manifestation of the inner self. As shown on Chart 1, the outer self includes both what it *is* and what it *does.* It *is* a physical body made up of organs or members. In addition, it is a brain or mental machine that thinks, understands, remembers, and so on. It is also a nervous system which is an amazing network that is neither totally physical nor nonphysical.

Contrary to what is often thought today, the outer self also includes our desires, emotions, and psychological urges, such as sex, fear, anger, curiosity, the love of beauty, ambition, and gregariousness (friendliness). *All* of these drives and emotions are *originally amoral.* They are neither good nor evil in and of themselves. We come into this world with desires that have no more moral character than the hunger for food. We must remember that.

But this outer self is also seen in what it *does.* It thinks and feels. To be sure, our thoughts and feelings can't be seen by other people, but they are seen by us and God. Then, when our thoughts and feelings are expressed in words and deeds, they can be and are seen by others.

This is what we are—within and without. There is an *inner* personhood that expresses itself through an *outer* personality.

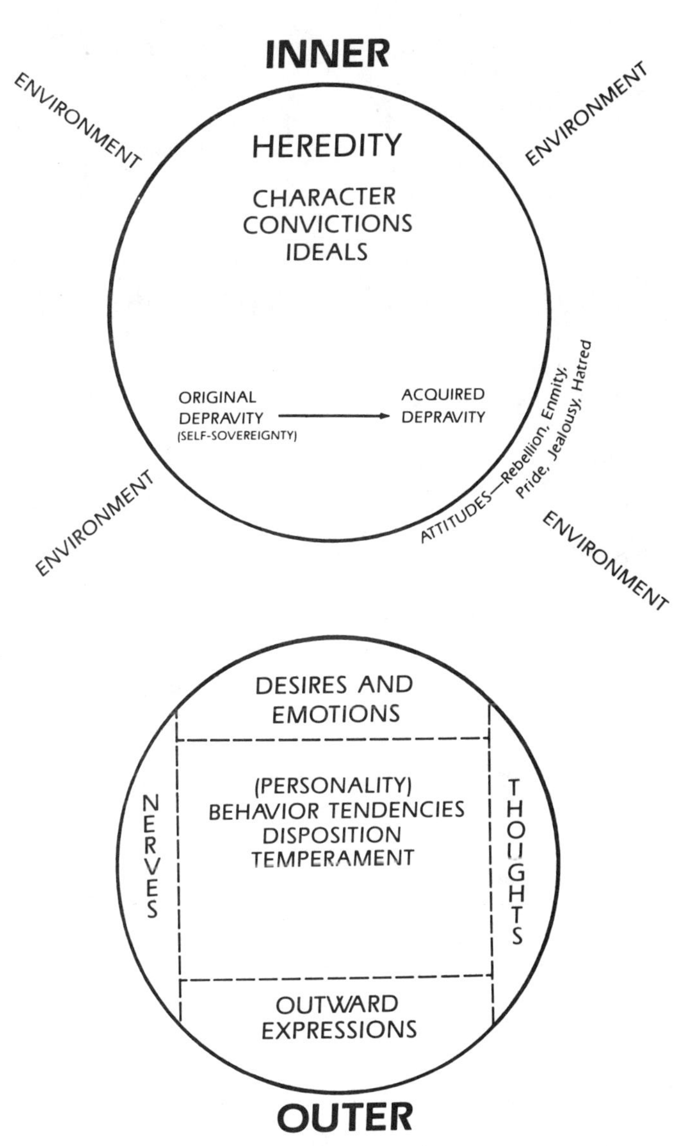

INNER
ENVIRONMENT
ENVIRONMENT
HEREDITY
CHARACTER
CONVICTIONS
IDEALS
ORIGINAL DEPRAVITY
(SELF-SOVEREIGNTY)
ACQUIRED DEPRAVITY
ATTITUDES—Rebellion. Enmity. Pride, Jealousy. Hatred
ENVIRONMENT
ENVIRONMENT
DESIRES AND EMOTIONS
NERVES
(PERSONALITY)
BEHAVIOR TENDENCIES
DISPOSITION
TEMPERAMENT
THOUGHTS
OUTWARD EXPRESSIONS
OUTER

9
What Makes Us What We Are?

Did you ever ask yourself, "Why am I what I am? What makes me this way?" On Chart 2 are shown three influences or factors that make us what we are *within*. They are heredity, environment, and (as all evangelicals believe) original sin.

The first-mentioned influence, heredity, is actually something we know very little about. We just know it happens. When the female egg is fertilized by the male sperm and conception takes place, life begins—shaped by a mysterious combination of genes. We haven't the faintest idea why certain ones come together and others don't. For years scientists have experimented with "genetic engineering," but they haven't helped us to understand this mystery.

We *do* know that heredity has a large part in determining what we are. We can readily see this in obvious physical characteristics such as stature, complexion, bone structure, facial appearance, and other features. It is intriguing that sometimes a dominant feature can lie dormant for a generation or more. Many times parents with blond and brunette hair have a child with red hair. A grandparent or great-grandparent, it turns out, had red hair.

Although a school of psychology may insist that behavioral characteristics are not hereditary, the obvious facts of life tell a different story. How often a child comes into our homes with a dominant personality or temperament trait that mystifies us. It could be stubbornness, rebelliousness, deceitfulness, extreme shyness, and so on. The variations are almost endless. We attempt to surround him with instruction, faithful example, and loving discipline; yet the problem persists. Our frustration is intensified when the child differs radically from our other children, almost like an ugly duckling. Sometimes the parents can see their child's problems mirrored in some of their own past personality conflicts. But that is often not the case. At other times the alien behavior can be related to a grandparent or even someone more distantly related. Yet many times the origin is a total mystery.

Why is this so important to recognize? It is because there are many parents who live for years with guilt because of an extremely difficult child. They feel personal responsibility for their child's failure, even though they earnestly tried to be faithful and consistent parents. More than one mother, because of training in behavioristic psychology, has shared with me a sense of guilt that has plagued her for years.

Of course it goes without saying that every parent has the sobering responsibility of providing for his child the best possible environment. And, sadly, too often this responsibility is tragically neglected. But we must remember that part of the reason we are what we are is due to heredity.

With heredity, however, environment is the second of the primary influences that make us what we are. The *training* and *teaching* received can have a great impact on us. When it is wholesome and good, the result is usually seen. On the other hand, the lack of correct training, or even injurious teaching, usually leaves its mark. *Examples* set before children can have a helpful or harmful effect. The *companions* they choose often determine the type of persons they become. Sometimes lives, even in later years, are deeply affected by either pleasant or tragic personal *experiences*. A pastor friend shared with me an incident concerning a young lady in his parish. She was suffering from deep trauma in her life. Only after several counseling sessions did my friend learn that some time earlier she had been brutally raped. That experience had deeply scarred her life.

Less dramatic, perhaps, but equally serious in their effects are the more general *circumstances* of life, such as poverty, educational deprivation, broken homes, criminal surroundings, and racial discrimination. All of these environmental factors help to form and shape our inner personhood.

In addition, as evangelicals we believe that every person is born into this world afflicted with original sin or depravity. There have been many efforts made to define and describe this spiritual malady, which can't be examined here. After several years of study, the clearest understanding that I have reached is what I call "self-sovereignty."[1] This explanation has been shared with literally thousands of people, and many have expressed gratitude and appreciation. Sovereignty means the power of control; thus understood, original sin causes everyone to enter this world in sovereign control of his own life. The sin of Adam and Eve was usurping the place in their lives that God has reserved for himself. They became lords of their own lives. In some way never fully understood, this assumption of God's prerogative has cursed the entire human race.

We are born with a bias, due to our perverted relationship with God. Psychologically, we have one center of reference—ourselves! Martin Luther described this as "being turned in on ourself and away from God." Our supreme passion is to satisfy ourselves. The consequence is that our minds are darkened (Rom. 1:28) and our hearts are hardened (2:5). In theological terms, our "original" depravity produces "acquired" depravity (cf. Chart 2). Inner attitudes such as rebellion, enmity, pride, jealousy, and hatred are developed.

It is important to recognize that such attitudes are *acquired.* We are not born that way. If we were, then we would be *morally* innocent of them. For instance, we are not born rebels, but we are born with the *capacity* of making ourselves such. That is just one frightening aspect of the curse of original sin.

This depraved inner self fashions and molds the *outer* self as an avenue of expression (cf. Chart 2). Our emotions and desires are shaped into a distinctive outer personality of behavioral tendencies, disposition, and temperament—*by the inner self.* We express outwardly what we are inwardly.

This is why we act like we do! All that can be seen by others is our personality mannerisms, moods, and idiosyncrasies. Expressions range all across the spectrum from moody to even tempered, lighthearted to serious, jovial to solemn, sensitive to callous, fussy to sloppy, stable to changeable, stubborn to vacillating, humorous to sober, friendly to distant, excitable to calm, talkative to quiet, impulsive to deliberate, thoughtful to unthinking, procrastinating to prompt, argumentative to agreeable, and so on. Such manifestations are simply an outward display of what we are inwardly.

But vastly more important than these dispositional characteristics is the way the sinner's outward life mirrors the depravity of his heart. His natural desires and appetites are warped and scarred into habit patterns of response, seeking to satisfy, or even satiate, his passion for self-indulgence. Also, his disposition or behavioral tendencies reflect the gratification of sinful and selfish desires. His normal human temperament is inflamed and abused—actually grooved and hardened into patterns of distinctive behavior.

Often we are told that it is of utmost importance to be saved when we are young. *Here is the greatest single reason why.* How urgent it is to come to Christ before years in sin have left their deep scars on our desires and affected our personality behavior.

Do you have a problem understanding how some people you know live such good lives and yet apparently feel no need for a vital experience with God? Through the years I have known several, but there is one family which particularly stands out in my mind. Bill and Jean were close and beautiful friends. There seemed to be nothing they would not do for Wini and me—and often demonstrated it. And we weren't the only ones! Many times I witnessed their loving concern for neighbors and friends. To my knowledge neither of them had any bad habits. In every observable way they lived conscientious and high-principled lives. However, they seldom went to church and expressed no need of God.

But my theology said they were sinners! They were part of the "all" who have sinned and fall short of the glory of God (Rom. 3:23). They made no profession of faith in Christ for salvation. Still "there is salvation in no one else; for there is no other name under heaven that has been given among men, by which we must be saved" (Acts 4:12). It troubled me. How could it be? There seemed to be no evidence of any adverse influences from the depraved heart with which we believe every person is born. Instead, Bill and Jean were examples of high personal standards, ideals, and convictions that put many of my professing Christian brethren to shame.

Of course we can never know all the intricate workings of any other person's life, even those closest to us. But we do know that sometimes the outward *expression* of inner attitudes is in great part determined by heredity and environment rather than original depravity. When a person is blessed with a refined heredity and wholesome environment, this can offset the influence of a sinful heart—*in outward actions.* Sinful impulses *can be* suppressed, at least temporarily. Consequently, the spiritual lack within is only revealed when there is a conflict between the human and divine will—as a challenge to the self. Also, when a person is depending on his good works for salvation, this often gives him an unusual motivation for behavior that matches a professing believer.

The puzzle never fully came together, but I had a greater

understanding when I met Jean's parents. They were devout followers of Christ. Their godly influence could be seen in their daughter. Such influence sometimes even reaches the "children's children." It taught me that it is never wise to attempt to make a surface comparison between a struggling believer and an exemplary unbeliever.

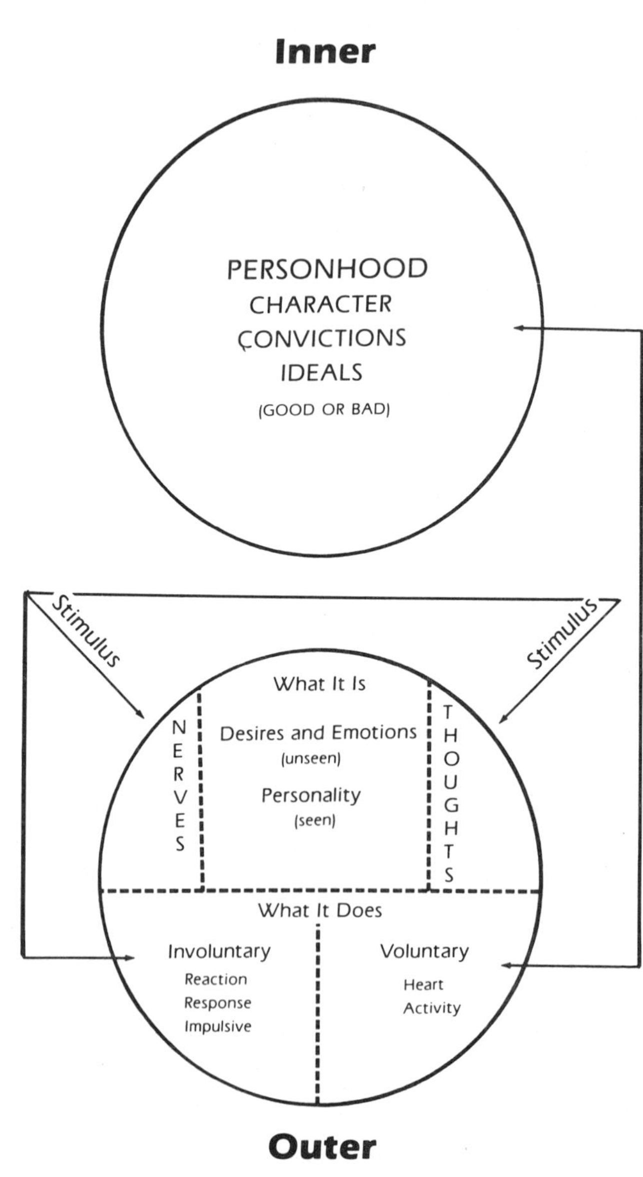

Inner
PERSONHOOD
CHARACTER
CONVICTIONS
IDEALS
(GOOD OR BAD)
Stimulus
Stimulus
What It Is
NERVES
Desires and Emotions
(unseen)
Personality
(seen)
THOUGHTS
What It Does
Involuntary
Reaction
Response
Impulsive
Voluntary
Heart
Activity
Outer

10
Why Did We Do It?

Have *you* ever asked the question: "Why did I do or say that?" What is the source or cause of your action? Often you really did not want or intend that it should happen.

The Bible makes a simple but very significant distinction about our actions. We can all easily understand it in our own experience. Some things we do or say come from our *hearts,* while other activity does not. Instead, we are simply *reacting* to stimuli in our environment. In more modern psychological terminology, the heart activity is *voluntarily* done with knowledge and will; and we are morally responsible for it. However, at other times our actions and words are unconscious or impulsive and completely involuntary *until after* they are done. Our response seems to be purely mechanical or automatic.

Certain types of reactive behavior, particularly in response to a physical stimulus, is relatively the same in everyone. Most of us react in the same way to a pinprick—we say, "Ouch." We duck to escape a threatened blow or blink when our eye is endangered. However, our reactions to other stimuli widely differ, depending upon our temperament or personality characteristics. The sudden appearance of a mouse will bring varied responses of fright, curiosity, or even attraction. Those viewing a tragic accident will react in many different ways—horror, silence, traumatic weeping, excited chatter, and so on.

Such reactions do not produce spiritual problems or questions. We simply accept them as a fact of life. But other reactions do! Under certain provocation, our impulsive behavior is not what we know it should be. Old habit patterns of desire or temperament, perhaps used for years to pamper or protect some self-centered ambition, almost automatically manifest themselves. After this happens we hurt and grieve.

As seen on Chart 3, we must clearly distinguish involuntary reaction from voluntary behavior. To fail to do so and instead lump them all together as sin, can only result in viewing all our behavior as helplessly sinful. This cuts the nerve of any effort to follow the biblical injunction to holy living. We certainly should lament our impulsive actions that are unchristian, and pursue every means possible to change them. However, such actions *need not produce guilt and condemnation.* God sees our hearts, and He knows our intentions and commitments.

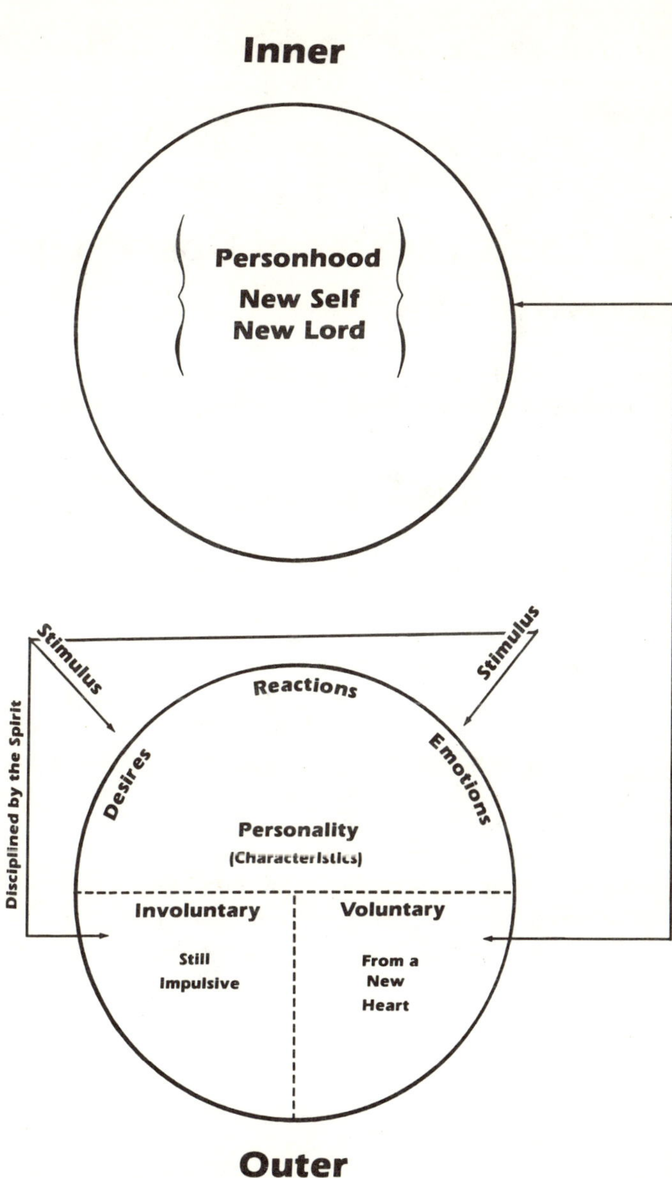

Inner
Personhood
New Self
New Lord
Stimulus
Stimulus
Reactions
Disciplined by the Spirit
Desires
Emotions
Personality
(Characteristics)
Involuntary
Voluntary
Still
Impulsive
From a
New
Heart
Outer

11

God's Theater of Operations

With this understanding of ourselves, we need to see how and where God works when we are saved and sanctified wholly. Exactly what is His theater of operations? It is in *the inner self or heart* (cf. Chart 4). Our inner personhood is dramatically changed.

But what about the outer self? What can God do there? We saw (cf. chap. 6) that the spiritual treasure in our heart is housed in an outer vessel that is weak and fragile. Nonetheless, this old outer self is the only means through which our new inner self can be expressed. We won't get a new body until the resurrection.

Does that mean that all our outward activity is hopelessly evil? Are we the helpless victims of sin? Certainly not! All that we do and say that comes from *the heart* should reflect our new personhood (cf. Chart 4). As new persons, with a new Lord, we can and must live new lives.

But what about our impulsive behavior? We saw (chap. 10) that our old personalities decidedly determine our involuntary reactions and responses. Old habit patterns of desire and temperament remain in our lives after we become a new person within. What can be done about them? Are we simply doomed to perpetual spiritual failure as long as we live in this old body? Is that what sinful depravity, a crucial point of evangelical theology, produces? The answer again is "Certainly not!"

As seen on Chart 4, through the discipline of the Spirit our impulsive behavior *can be changed.* This, too, must be the theater of God's operations. Our desires and emotions, as well as our personality characteristics, can be disciplined by the Holy Spirit. We will explore this in the remainder of our study.

We can now more plainly see why a biblical understanding of ourselves, technically termed *anthropology,* is so important. Many evangelicals view original sin as existing in the *outer man.* If this were so, no deliverance from its power would be possible while we live in this world. But such a totally pessimistic outlook is not what we see in the New Testament. Thank God! We shall see there is help and hope for us while we live in these bodies, even though they are "earthen vessels."

PART IV—WHAT CAN BE DONE?

We have had a good and honest look at the problem: How can we put together God's requirement that we live a holy life with the sometimes painful fact of our humanness—weaknesses, failures, personality faults, and so on? We are beginning to understand ourselves in biblical terms—why we think and act like we do. Now we come to the BIG question: *Can anything be done about it?*

As we seek more perfectly to *express outwardly* (in our lives) what we have *experienced inwardly* (in our hearts), two areas of failure can be identified (cf. Chart 5). One battleground, *hidden* from the view of others, is our warfare with physical desires and psychological drives that have been misused while living in sin. It is very easy to get temptation and sin mixed up in our minds, causing great spiritual anxiety.

The other battleground is outwardly *visible* and many times glaringly so! All of us have habit patterns of impulsive behavior which express our distinctive personalities and temperaments. It is true, thank God, that He knows our hearts. He understands what we meant to do or say. But people don't see our hearts; they only see what has happened. They don't know if our actions came from our hearts or were largely involuntary reactions, accompanied by little or no thought.

We shall examine these two areas of difficulty and seek to discover how God can help us. But first, we need to look at some related questions.

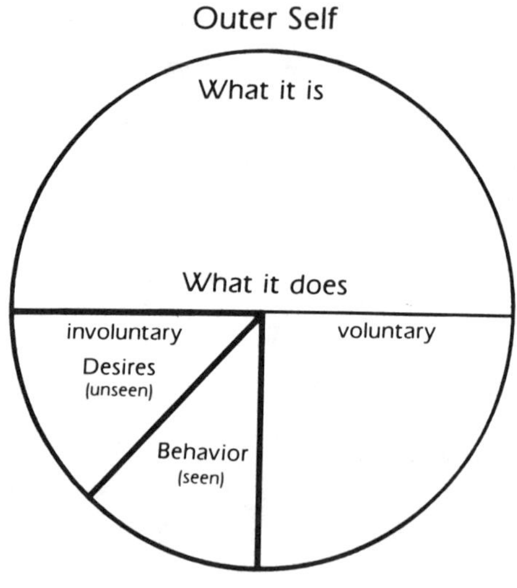

12
Some Wrong Ideas

Many outside the Wesleyan tradition often accuse us of teaching and professing "sinless perfection." By this they mean complete perfection of performance. To my knowledge, no responsible Wesleyan scholar has ever made this claim. John Wesley himself repeatedly refused to use the term *sinless perfection.* Those who suggest that Wesleyans preach such a doctrine of perfection only disclose their own lack of understanding.[1] Unfortunately, at times this is a straw man that can easily be set up and demolished.

Our concern, however, is with those who consider themselves Wesleyans. Sometimes they also have wrong ideas. What does entire sanctification do for us (cf. chap. 5)? What does it mean to live a holy life? There is a great deal of misunderstanding right here.

As so often happens in life, there are two extremes. Some are convinced that entire sanctification solves all of their problems. If they experience spiritual failure, they feel a need to go back to the altar. They are certain that those who are really sanctified don't have such defeats.

Once as a pastor I was attempting to minister to Ruth, a young wife who was contemplating divorce. Her great difficulty was the inconsistency of her husband, Joe. She was convinced he was a hypocrite. Although he was a highly respected and greatly loved leader in the church, his life at home was another story. He would become impatient, irritated, and upset with her. At times he made things very difficult. After carefully explaining some of the things we have been examining, she found a place of faith and peace. We agreed to pray urgently for Joe. I knew him well enough to realize that I could not directly talk to him about the problem. So when we decided to discuss the subject of holiness and human frailty at a zone ministers' meeting, I thought it would be an ideal time to deal with the issue. Joe went to the meeting with me and carefully listened to the discussion, which was sometimes heated. On our way home I anxiously waited for his reaction. He explained to me that he always tried to be open minded. Thus, he was quite willing to accept the fact that some people could only find help by discipline and struggle. But with no great sense of pride, Joe testified: "When God sanctified me, He took care of all that."

Was Joe a hypocrite? I am convinced that he wasn't. Instead, he was simply blind to what was glaringly obvious, especially to his wife. Sometimes we have here a serious psychological complication. If we have been taught that sanctification will eliminate a certain type of behavior, then it is very easy to convince ourselves that this kind of behavior doesn't exist. We can develop a mental block so that *we really do not see* what others do. Sadly, many have been unjustly accused of hypocrisy when their problem was blindness to their own shortcomings. We are often the last ones to realize our own failures.

Although such persons *theoretically* deny perfection of performance, saying, "No one is perfect," they often *practically* expect perfect performance *in certain areas.* They simply conclude that if one is sanctified there will not be failure in that sphere of living. When there is, then the only solution known is "another trip to the altar" to get sanctified again.

There is also a reaction to the conflict we have been examining *at the opposite extreme.* For some, the problem *is* seen, but they are convinced there is no solution. The attitude is often expressed: "God made me this way, it is simply me, and I can't do anything about it. Furthermore, God loves and understands me; and if people don't, that is just too bad, and they will have to put up with me."

The sad part of both extremes—self-blindness or helplessness—is that the problem is never dealt with. Many distressing and even heartbreaking stories can be told of deeply sincere and greatly talented persons whose lives and usefulness have been seriously hampered by personality and temperament frailties.

Certainly God has help for all of us here. As we prayerfully open our hearts to Him, He will reveal to us the wonders of His grace.

13
What About Our Body?

Let's be sure we know what the Bible means by the earthly body. In the simplest sense it is all that will one day remain on earth when we leave (cf. chap. 8). It is the outer self through which the inner self is expressed in this world. In more modern terms, it is *both* physical and psychological. Paul called it our "outer man" (*exō anthrōpos*, 2 Cor. 4:16), "earthly house" (*epigeios oikia*, 5:1, KJV), and "tent" or "tabernacle" (*skēnos*, 5:1, 4, KJV). What does the New Testament tell us about this human house?

At first appearance the New Testament teaching looks like a strange paradox, if not a contradiction. How easy it is to be hung up on one horn of what seems to be a dilemma. There is no question but that the hope of the gospel is the *resurrection of the body.* We are going to have a new body; that much is clear from Paul's vivid metaphors. This old body will one day be *redeemed* (Rom. 8:23). Only this will complete the redemptive provision of the Cross. In addition, our present body will be *exchanged* for "a building from God, a house not made with hands, eternal in the heavens" (2 Cor. 5:1). Also, the body we live in today will be dramatically *changed.*

So also is the resurrection of the dead. It is sown a perishable body, it is raised an imperishable body; it is sown in dishonor, it is raised in glory; it is sown in weakness, it is raised in power; it is sown a natural body, it is raised a spiritual body. If there is a natural body, there is also a spiritual body. . . . Behold, I tell you a mystery; we shall not all sleep, but we shall all be changed, in a moment, in the twinkling of an eye, at the last trumpet; for the trumpet will sound, and the dead will be raised imperishable, and we shall be changed. For this perishable must put on the imperishable, and this mortal must put on immortality. But when this perishable will have put on the imperishable, and this mortal will have put on immortality, then will come about the saying that is written, "DEATH IS SWALLOWED UP in victory" (1 Cor. 15:42-44, 51-54).

And finally, this earthly body will be *transformed*.

For our citizenship is in heaven, from which also we eagerly wait for a Savior, the Lord Jesus Christ; who will transform the body of our humble state into conformity with the body of His glory, by the exertion of the power that He has even to subject all things to Himself (Phil. 3:20-21).

Without question this is the living hope of the new man in Christ, from the 1st century to the 20th century. Particularly in times of test and trial, multiplied millions have been sustained by the glorious prospect of personal resurrection. Its expectation has been the heartthrob of the Christian Church. Without it man's faith has become dim and even been destroyed.

Yet no less clear is another thread of teaching in the New Testament. While we await that blessed day of resurrection, God expects us to live a holy life—in these present bodies that are mortal and "corruptible" (KJV). As Paul sought to show the Corinthians the great evil of immorality, he wrote them:

Yet the body is not for immorality, but for the Lord; and the Lord is for the body. . . . Do you not know that your bodies are members of Christ? Shall I then take away the members of Christ and make them members of a harlot? May it never be! (1 Cor. 6:13, 15).

He went on to point out that "your body is a temple of the Holy Spirit" (v. 19). The result is that "you have been bought with a price: therefore *glorify God in your body*" (v. 20, italics added). Again, in a later letter to these same Corinthians, as the Apostle sought to warn them against a corrupting attachment to their wicked world, he wrote: "Or what agreement has the temple of God with idols? For we are the temple of the living God" (2 Cor. 6:16).

Jesus himself referred to His body as a temple (cf. Mark 14:58; John 2:19, 21). Can there be any doubt that He meant the temple of God? The truth of the Incarnation is that His body is the same as ours, without the scars of sin.

Probably the most challenging aspect of all is the witness of Paul that in spite of severe tests and trials, *the life of Jesus was manifested in his body,* or mortal flesh (cf. 2 Cor. 4:10-11). Do we realize what the significance of "to be manifest" (*phaneroō)* is? It means "to reveal" or "to be made known." When people look at us, in these bodies, *they should see that Christ is alive in us!* That sounds like a mighty high, even unattainable, standard of living, but can anything less be our objective in the light of Scripture?

Paul had still more incredible things to say about these earthly bodies. He exhorted the Roman believers to no longer "present" (*paristēmi)* the members of their bodies to the enslaving power of sin. Instead, now that they had been freed from sin's slavery, he urged them to present their members as instruments, even as slaves, of righteousness to God (Rom. 6:13, 19). In another graphic picture Paul appealed to them to present their bodies to God as a sacrifice. "I urge you therefore, brethren, by the mercies of God, to present your bodies a living and holy sacrifice, acceptable to God which is your spiritual service of worship" (12:1).

It is difficult for us to realize what that meant in that day. The prevailing Greek idea was that the earthly body was intrinsically and helplessly evil. It was a hopeless prison house of sin from which the soul must escape. But, based on the Jewish view of man, New Testament teaching rejected this attitude toward the body. *In fact, the first major heresy that infant church faced was over this very issue.* Unfortunately, already in New Testament times there were tendencies that crystalized in the philosophical system of Gnosticism[1] in the second century. The apologists, climaxing with Irenaeus, branded this view of the body as heretical. Amazingly, however, some evangelicals still today write off the present body as evil and a handicap that makes holy living impossible. The teaching of the New Testament that speaks of *being* holy, while still living in the body, is ignored. At best, holiness is in "standing" and not "living."

How are we to put together these two strands of New Testament teaching on the body—a future hope but also a present responsibility? The answer is that this old body is to be *disciplined* by the Holy Spirit as we live by His power. God expects us to live disciplined lives. Our major problem is that we are part of a sadly undisciplined generation. We are much more accustomed to self-indulgence.

14
Living Under Discipline

What does it mean to live a disciplined life? It certainly is *not asceticism*. Particularly in Paul's day, asceticism lays at the heart of most religions, specifically with regard to living a holy life. The basic idea was that a person became increasingly holy by self-denial, sacrifice, and suffering. The more severely he punished himself, for God's sake of course, the holier he became. In many Eastern religions "holy men" would, and still do, walk on spikes and red-hot coals or undergo many types of self-torture. Before Martin Luther discovered the great truth that "the just shall live by faith" (Rom. 1:17, KJV), he almost physically destroyed himself in an Augustinian monastery—trying to make himself holy.

Paul had to combat this error, especially in the Colossian church.

> If you have died with Christ to the elementary principles of the world, why, as if you were living in the world, do you submit yourself to decrees, such as, "Do not handle, do not taste, do not touch!" (which all refer to things destined to perish with the using)—in accordance with the commandments and teachings of men? These are matters which have, to be sure, the appearance of wisdom in self-made religion and self-abasement and severe treatment of the body, but are of no value against fleshly indulgence *(Col. 2:20-23)*.

The necessary discipline for a holy life must not be confused with the "works righteousness" of asceticism.

Neither is the discipline needed in our lives a form of *legalism.* We *can be* disciplined by the "lash of the law." Under its cracking whip there is a form of regulation and restriction—do this, don't do that, go here, don't go there, and so on. But Paul would have been the last person in the world to advocate that Gentiles should live under such law. He knew, by experience, the wretchedness and moral frustration of legalism.

The simple fact is that we can't discipline ourselves enough to live a truly holy life! We will end up living by the flesh, which Paul knew was spiritually fatal. Sometimes the vivid picture of discipline in his own life has been understood as such self-discipline, even a form of asceticism.

> Do you not know that those who run in a race all run, but only one receives the prize? Run in such a way that you may win. And everyone who competes in the games exercises self-control in all things. They do it to receive a perishable wreath, but we an imperishable. Therefore I run in such a way, as not without aim; I box in such a way, as not beating the air; but I buffet my body and make it my slave, lest possibly, after I have preached to others, I myself should be disqualified (*1 Cor. 9:24-27*).

However this exhortation and testimony must be understood in its crucial context. First, it is necessary to remember Paul's difficult task throughout the *entire* first Corinthian letter. He dealt with several critical problems.[1] A large part of the difficulty was that they were a very undisciplined people. In the ninth chapter, Paul sought to challenge them with the discipline of his own life. The Corinthian believers, among many other things, were jealously defending their "rights"—specifically their right to freedom or liberty. This was causing problems. Paul reminded them that he had several "rights" as an apostle—of diet, marriage, church support, and so on. But he had freely chosen not to exercise any of them.

He explained the "glory of the unrequired." God's greatest blessings did not come from doing what was required or from claiming his rights. Instead, as he served God by voluntarily denying himself and doing what he did not have to do, he found his Lord's greatest blessings. Thus, "though I am free from all men, I have made myself a slave to all, that I might win the more. . . . And I do all things for the sake of the gospel, that I may become a fellow partaker of it" (1 Cor. 9:19, 23).

In an area about which the Corinthians were most contentious, eating meat offered to idols, Paul applied this vital discipline. Although he knew that meat from an idol sacrifice was not unclean or morally contaminated (cf. 8; 10:19), yet he personally lived under the discipline of love. "Therefore, if food causes my brother to stumble, I will never eat meat again, that I might not cause my brother to stumble" (8:13).

This is the context for Paul's graphic illustration of the discipline practiced in the Greek athletic festivals quoted above. Undoubtedly, he was alluding to the famous Isthmian games at Corinth, second in prominence only to the Olympics. They were held every two years. With dramatic imagery Paul contrasted the athletes' rigorous discipline to gain a perishable crown (a laurel wreath) with the Christian's necessary discipline to win the imperishable crown of eternal life. Specifically, Paul illustrated this discipline by references to not running in circles or shadow boxing, but instead "beating up" (lit., giving himself a black eye) his *body* so that he would not be disqualified from life's crucial race. His pointed allusion to body discipline was probably a response to the intense temptation to sensual sins in Corinth.[2]

But where did the "love" (*agapē*) that was the dynamic of Paul's discipline come from? It was, of course, the fruit of the Spirit! The Apostle knew so well that the disciplined life was only possible by the Spirit. Actually, "self-control" *(egkrateia)* was listed by him among the Spirit's fruit (Gal. 5:23). Here is his alternative to living under the lash of the law. The believer can and must know the "link of love" as he walks by the Spirit. Love is the greatest single disciplinary force in the world, and that love is not human love at all. God, who loves us, would love *through* us! As we walk through life together, He would lovingly discipline us, directing and correcting us with tender compassion.

This is something the Judaizers, especially in Galatia, never understood. The discipline of the Spirit is a crucial safeguard against both legalism and license.

Unfortunately, many today fail to understand Paul's crucial distinction between living by the *law* and living under the discipline of *principles.* It is true, thank God, that we are freed from the enslaving bondage of the law through faith in Christ. *Legalism is not Christian!* There is a blessed emancipation from its bondage, in Christian freedom. But that does not mean we are free to do *our* "thing." Rather, we are set free to do *His* "thing." There is a BIG difference.

In this same Corinthian letter Paul explicitly says: "All things are lawful for me" (1 Cor. 6:12; cf. 10:23). But does that mean he had total license to live as he desired? Certainly not! *In that same Corinthian letter* Paul repeatedly limited freedom by several vital principles, related to doing and being. The basic ones were: *doing* what is spiritually necessary or profitable (1 Cor. 6:12; 10:23), *not doing* what would master him (6:12), *being* God's holy temple (v. 19), and *doing* what is for our neighbor's good (10:24). Lest there be any misunderstanding, Paul repeatedly stated that there are some things a believer *can't do and get to heaven* (cf. 1 Cor. 6:9-10; Gal. 5:21; Eph. 5:5; Col. 3:5-6).

However, the principles that Paul listed were not laws. Instead, they provided a necessary discipline. In fact, upon closer examination we see that they all are specific applications of love. They are what James, but not Paul, called the "perfect law" (1:25), the "royal law" (2:8), and the "law of liberty" (1:25; 2:12).

How sad to confuse the love *(agapē)* of the New Testament with what is called love today, which is often indulgent, permissive, grasping, and demanding. Such is simply selfishness. Divine love, a fruit of the Spirit, is the direct opposite. Instead of true Christian freedom leading to sinful license, it results in disciplined living. By the Spirit, that love provides principles for practical living.

The specific principles that we have been discussing are only suggestive. Our task is to find by the Holy Spirit the principles revealed to us in Scripture and then follow them. As we do, they will provide for us the dynamic for disciplined living.

15
The Negative Is Never the End

Unfortunately, the word *discipline* has a negative image for many of us. It makes us think of punishment or prohibition ("You can't do this or that!"). And it *is* true that sometimes discipline involves a "spanking." Just as we needed it physically as a child, it is spiritually necessary as we are growing up. A "trip to the woodshed" for spiritual discipline is a vital part of our training. It helps us to remember that God's chastening is "for our own good."

But only to look at discipline as punishment misses what is most important. God, as a loving parent, is trying to shape and mold us. He wants us to be like Jesus! That is the purpose of discipline and includes doing the right as well as not doing the wrong.

In the New Testament a very graphic word is used to describe disciplined living (cf. Acts 21:24; Rom. 4:12; Gal. 5:25; 6:16; Phil. 3:16). *Stoicheō* literally means "to be kept in line" or "to walk by a rule or standard." Much of its meaning is lost in many English versions when it is translated simply as "walk," like the more common word for walking *(peripateō)*—cf. Gal. 5:16 with 5:25. It is a military term and is perhaps best translated "march." So Paul exhorts the Galatian believers to not only "walk" *(peripateō)* but to "march" *(stoicheō)* by the Spirit. "If by the (Holy) Spirit we have our life [in God], let us go forward *walking in line,* our conduct controlled by the Spirit" (Gal. 5:25, Amp., italics added). Marching by the Spirit certainly is guidance in the *right* way as well as correction of the *wrong* way.[1]

Yet *there is a legitimate and necessary negative element in discipline.* Sometimes, when we are freed from the bondage of totally negative restrictions, the "pendulum swing" goes into operation. We swing to the opposite extreme and reject *all* negative concepts. This is particularly a problem today with the sometimes overpowering emphasis on positive thinking, which *categorically denies any value in even a negative thought.* Such an attitude misses much of the New Testament and can only be embraced by rationalizing away a vital part of it.

There are many negatives in the Bible. And not simply in the Old Testament! Without doubt we think first of the Ten Commandments. However, we must remember that Jesus emphasized "the commandments." He told the rich young ruler: "You know the commandments" (Luke 18:20). It is impossible to take seriously the teaching of Jesus, starting with the Sermon on the Mount (Matthew 5—7), without seeing a great many negative statements. Paul also had much to say about negative restrictions. He warned of the "works of the flesh" (Gal. 5:19-21) and exhorted the Colossians to "put away" anger, wrath, malice, slander, and abusive speech (Col. 3:8-9; also Eph. 4:25-32; 5:3-7). These are only a few examples. But that is *not* the whole story!

The same Jesus told the rich young ruler some *positive* things to do—go, sell, give, come, follow Me. If all you find in the Sermon on the Mount is negative ideas, you miss its central message—love, pray, give, forgive, seek, trust, and so on. Of course the most significant word of all is Jesus' interpretation of the greatest commandment:

"AND YOU SHALL LOVE THE LORD YOUR GOD WITH ALL YOUR HEART, AND WITH ALL YOUR SOUL, AND WITH ALL YOUR MIND, AND WITH ALL YOUR STRENGTH. The second is this, "YOU SHALL LOVE YOUR NEIGHBOR AS YOURSELF." There is no other commandment greater than these *(Mark 12:30-31).*

Likewise the same Paul spoke of the "fruit of the Spirit" —immediately after listing the "deeds of the flesh" (Gal. 5:19-23). He also exhorted the Colossians to "put on a heart of compassion, kindness, humility, gentleness and patience; . . . And beyond all these things put on love, which is the perfect bond of unity" (Col. 3:12-14). He urged the Ephesians:

> And be kind to one another, tender-hearted, forgiving each other, just as God in Christ also has forgiven you. Therefore be imitators of God, as beloved children; and walk in love, just as Christ also loved you, and gave Himself up for us, an offering and a sacrifice to God as a fragrant aroma *(Eph. 4:32—5:2).*

I have many times asked myself what is the most significant thing I have learned from many years of studying Pauline thought. It could very well be his repeated emphasis that *the negative is never the end.* Negatives are important—yes, absolutely necessary; yet they are never the last word. For Paul, as for Jesus, *the negative is always the stepping-stone to the positive.* And, of course, the positive both begins and climaxes in love.

As we examine what can be done about the old outer self, through which the new inner self must be expressed, we must remember this New Testament relationship between the negative and positive. Much needed discipline is based upon this vital relationship.

Paul beautifully and explicitly expressed this at a crucial point in his important Roman letter. It was after his thorough treatment of the *total sinfulness* of man (Rom. 1:16—3:20) and God's wondrous plan of *total redemption* (3:21—8:39). Then, following an interlude about the tragedy of Israel (Romans 9—11), the Apostle made some very pointed and urgent admonitions about the holy life (Romans 12—15). This "practics section," as it has been called, begins with:

> I urge you therefore, brethren, by the mercies of God, to present your bodies a living and holy sacrifice, acceptable to God, which is your spiritual service of worship. And *do not be conformed* to this world, but *be transformed* by the renewing of your mind, that you may prove what the will of God is, that which is good and acceptable and perfect *(Rom. 12:1-2, italics added).*

Obviously, verse 1 picks up the theme that he previously had stated. Then, in verse 2, he exhorted them to the disciplined living that must follow the crisis presentation. First the *negative*—"do not be conformed"! It literally means "to be fashioned by the age." Resist the pull of this age that would pull you under and fashion you to its evil spirit. J. B. Phillips' translation is classic: "Don't let the world around you squeeze you into its own mold."

Then follows the *positive* counterpart: "But be transformed by the renewing of your mind." Paul's choice of words is dramatic. "Be transformed" is the Greek term *metamorphoō,* which we transliterate as *metamorphosis.* Transformation always is a process, as is so beautifully pictured in the metamorphosis of a caterpillar into a butterfly. In addition, *every time* the New Testament speaks of human transformation the progressive Greek tense is used (present tense).[2]

Here is the pattern of disciplined living—by the Spirit. We shall see the negative and positive elements blended, with the negative never the end.

PART V—MISUSED DESIRES DISCIPLINED

Our outer self was sculptured by our old inner self. What we *are* on the outside was shaped by what we *were* on the inside (cf. chap. 9). We saw that a critical part of the outer self consisted of our desires, both physical appetites and psychological drives. Although these are in the outer man (cf. chaps. 8—9, Charts 1 and 2), they are unseen by anyone but ourselves. When we seek to live a holy life we come face-to-face with desires that we know are improper. Consequently, there is often a hidden struggle and even desperation in our lives. What can we do? Is there relief from this lonely battle?

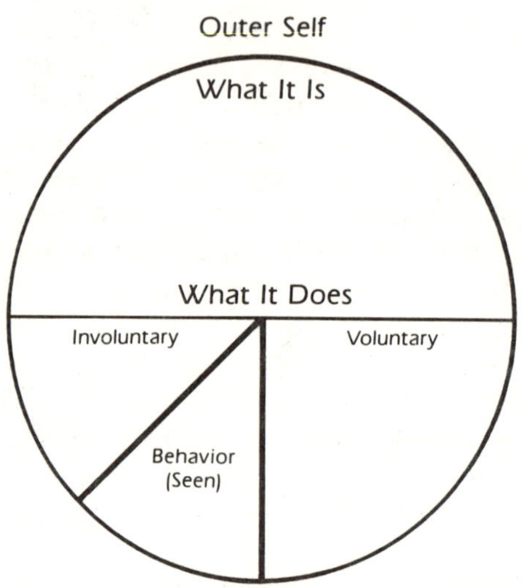

Outer Self
What It Is
What It Does
Involuntary
Voluntary
Behavior
(Seen)

16
What Is Desire?

We need to start here—with a clear understanding of what desire is. Many of us are confused, discouraged, and even spiritually defeated because of a lack of clarity. Many times a suggestion, or even a promise, is given in a sermon that in the experience of entire sanctification all of our sinful desires will be taken away. Well, that all depends upon what is meant! With total honesty we can give ourselves completely to God. But then, when we are faced with temptation, the old desires *are still there.* What is wrong? Where have we failed? Was our commitment incomplete?

Part of the problem is careless and unscriptural preaching. As ministers of the gospel we cannot be too prudent in dealing with the souls to whom we minister. A thoughtless comment from the pulpit can easily cause irreparable harm. Of prime importance is diligence to be true to our basic authority—the Scriptures. Often confusion about the removal of desires stems from a failure to understand the crucial New Testament distinction between the inner and outer self (cf. chap. 8). When we speak about a total change of desires, do we mean those in our heart or in our psychological-physical bodies, the "outer man"?

What complicates our understanding is the obviously ambiguous usage of the word "desire" today. By "desire" we can mean the *attitude* of our inner self. But often we mean by the term the *appetite* of the outer self. So, when we speak about desires being changed, it is of greatest importance to determine exactly what we mean.

Thank God, our *inner attitudes* are changed in salvation! In that sense we no longer "desire" or "want" to do what is wrong or sinful. An old-time country preacher said it effectively: "The things I once hated I now love, and the things I once loved I now hate." This speaks of an *inner* attitude or desire.

But our *outward appetites* are not changed as an intrinsic part of salvation. As noted in chapter 11, we can only express our *new* heart through our *old* body. This includes what we can properly call "desires," both physical and psychological.

Thus, what does salvation do with regard to our desires? God takes away the old inner desire (attitude) to satisfy the outer desires (appetites) in the wrong way. But the old outer desires still remain! Does that mean that sin is inevitable? We shall see that God can do more than that for us.

17
Temptation or Sin?

The failure to distinguish clearly between temptation and sin causes great spiritual anxiety and even soul agony. Temptation is only possible *through our desires!* The Synoptics (Matthew, Mark, and Luke) all record the temptations of Jesus in the wilderness of Judea.[1] There was only one way that Jesus could have been tempted, and that was through His desires. Don't you think He was hungry when the devil suggested that He make the stones into bread? Those small, flat stones on a hillside looked—and probably even smelled—like fresh loaves of bread as they come out of a warm oven. Fasting for 40 days and nights does something to a man's imagination. And Jesus was a man with desires identical to ours.

James gave us a vivid picture of exactly how temptation works and how it can become sin:

> But each one is tempted when he is carried away and enticed by his own lust. Then when lust has conceived, it gives birth to sin; and when sin is accomplished, it brings forth death *(James 1:14-15).*

I like to call this "the life cycle of sin."

How does temptation happen? It occurs when our own "desires" are carried away and enticed. It is most unfortunate that so many English versions translate the Greek word *epithumia* as "lust." As any Greek lexicon will show, that is not its basic meaning. It simply means "desire" with no suggestion of it being good *or* bad intrinsically, in and of itself. In fact, the term *(epithumia)* is used of *good* desires, even the desires of the Spirit.[2] What is so crucial is that "lust" today carries the connotation, for most people, of an evil desire (cf. NIV translation of this verse).

If temptation is only possible through an evil desire, then Jesus could never have been tempted! But we know that He both was tempted and did not have evil desires. The fact is that He was tempted just like we are. "For we do not have a high priest who cannot sympathize with our weaknesses, but one who has been tempted in all things as we are, yet without sin" (Heb. 4:15). Could it be clearer? We don't have to have evil desires to be tempted. We simply have to have desires.

James said we are tempted when we are "carried away and enticed" by our desires. Perhaps we can understand this better if we think of our desires being stimulated, quickened, or awakened. They merely react to the stimuli that is placed before them. This is the principle that lies behind all fishing. The successful fisherman discovers what bait will attract the fish he is seeking to catch. In a sense he is "tempting" the fish.

It is significant that in this graphic description of temptation Satan is never mentioned, although we always associate him with it. We should make the association because he *is* the "tempter." Even though unmentioned, his role in all temptation is clear. It is Satan's task to see to it that the most appealing "bait" is placed before us. He knows exactly what will be the most attractive to us, and he does his work well. Too often we forget that the same thing does not tempt all people. What might have a great appeal to one person could very well be of no interest to another. No place is the awareness of this fact so vital as when we seek to minister to young people. We speak of the "generation gap" today, and by it we mean that there are two entirely different realms of interest and even values. Often we seem to be living in different worlds! A vital part of this is in the sphere of desire. The normal young person simply does not have the same desires as an older person. We need to remember this as our youth struggle with their temptations. They may seem of little consequence to those of us who are older.

We must realize that stimulated desire is not sin. It is just temptation. James said: "Each one is *tempted.*" *For our desires to be awakened by an enticement does not mean we have sinned.* We are simply being tempted. This is at the impulsive level. As seen above in chapter 10, one of the reasons why we act, and even think, like we do is that we react impulsively to the stimuli of our environment.

With another graphic metaphor, or word picture, James went on to show how temptation *could* become sin. "Then when lust [desire] has conceived, it gives birth to sin" (James 1:15). This image is drawn from the manner in which all life begins. When the female egg is fertilized by the male sperm, conception takes place and life commences. So—*only* when our stimulated desire joins with "something else" is sin born. What is that "something else"? It is our *will!* Stimulated desire united with our will brings sin into being. Stimulated desire *alone* is only temptation; but when it is yoked to our will, sin is created.

Then James gave the final chapter in the life cycle of sin: "And when sin is accomplished, it brings forth death" (James 1:15). The translation "accomplished" does not adequately complete James's graphic picture. The Greek term is *apoteleō,* which literally means to "complete." In James's figure, the completion of life is to be fully grown or grown up. What a gripping description! Sin is born as a tiny, innocent, helpless infant. But when it is full grown, it produces death! How tragically true!

It is of greatest importance that we understand the difference between temptation and sin as we seek to learn how to discipline our desires. Sadly, many have suffered a lifelong guilt trip because of not making such a distinction. Only God knows how many have become spiritual casualties because of this confusion. As suggested in chapter 16, this is often caused by careless and unscriptural preaching that promises the purification or remaking of all desires in salvation.

This is why we dare not live to satisfy or fulfill our *own* desires—even after we are saved. Tragically, the sainted Augustine has often been quoted (out of context): "Love God and do what you please." *He was not speaking of our bodily desires or appetites.* He had more sense than that!

Paul made it pointedly clear that we dare not do what we please. He said: "But I say, walk by the Spirit, and you will not carry out the desire of the flesh" (Gal. 5:16). Then, as grounds for such a claim, he went on in the next verse: "For these [desires of the flesh and Spirit] are in opposition to one another *so that you may not do the things that you please*" (v. 17, italics added).[3] The only way we can abstain from doing what we please (or desire) is by the power of the Holy Spirit. That is why Paul's repeated exhortation is *not* to "give opportunity to the flesh" (v. 13), "sow to the flesh" (6:8), or "make provision for the flesh" (Rom. 13:14). This is because it is in the flesh that our passions and desires are located (cf. Gal. 5:24).

Closely related to what we think of as desires are our thoughts. There is a *real* difference between a thought that Satan puts in our minds as a *suggestion,* and our *willful acceptance* of that thought. When a thought comes to the level of consciousness, we have a moral decision to make: We can reject and disown it, or we can accept it and make it our own. The ancient proverb contains a lot of wisdom: "You can't keep the birds from flying over your head, but you don't need to let them build a nest in your hair."

One area of intense struggle in today's sex-saturated society is with our sexual drives and urges. Unfortunately, it has

sometimes been suggested that if our hearts have been puri-
fied, we will be totally unmoved by any illicit sexual stimulation. Thus, if and when we are confronted by indecency
and degrees of nudity—perhaps on the TV or billboard, in
magazines, or even just walking down the street!—our sex
drive will be totally unaffected and unmoved. In such a view
the mere arousing of desire is sin. This hopelessly confuses
temptation and sin. Stimulated desire is not sin but is merely
temptation.

However, there *is* a crucial line of distinction. In spite of
the popularity of "girl watching"—even in sometime "proper" society—Jesus made it plain that looking can become sin.
"But I say to you, that everyone who looks on a woman to lust
for her has commited adultery with her already in his heart"
(Matt. 5:28). What is that line of distinction? *It is your will!*
Sometimes we cannot escape seeing—and even experiencing
sexual stimulation—but if and when it becomes *willful gawk-
ing,* sin results.

Perhaps this examination of temptation and sin has
seemed to be unnecessarily explicit. But in order for us to
experience the discipline of misused desires, we first must
clearly understand the difference between temptation and
sin.

18
What Sin Leaves Behind

What was described in the last chapter is in many ways hypothetical. I attempted to distinguish between temptation and sin on the basis of desires *unaffected by sin.* This condition *can* exist in those who were saved while they were young, before sin had an opportunity to wreak its havoc. What I tried to show is that such persons, when they strive to live holy lives, have a struggle with temptation because of the very nature of desire itself.

But for most of us that is not the case. What does sin leave behind? Often its legacy is a body that has been ravaged and tyrannized. While living in sin, our desires were misused and abused. Legitimate desires were given illegitimate satisfaction. Because of inward depravity, we had one center of reference—ourselves. Our prime obsession was self-satisfaction. For some this was not only gratification but a banquet of indulgence.

What happened to the desires with which we were born that were neither good nor bad? They lost their innocence or moral neutrality. They *became* evil and inclined in the wrong direction. They were warped and scarred, even so grooved that they became a channel of expression for our depraved heart. When stimulated, they impulsively responded to please, indulge, pamper, and even protect our inner self. There was built up a habit pattern of response or compulsive behavior.

In fact, it *seemed* like new evil desires were created. But sin does not create new desires. *Only God can create!* Sin can and did misuse and corrupt the natural desires we already had. Every single work of the flesh is a corruption of a potentially good desire (Gal. 5:19-21). There could have been a right fulfillment, but the legitimate was used in an illegitimate manner.

Sometimes what appears to be a new desire is an intensification, through abuse, of a *single* appetite. If one indulged in promiscuous sex while living a sinful life, his normal sex drive can be so inflamed that its satisfaction becomes a consuming obsession. At other times a combination of desires is involved. Physical appetites, such as hunger and thirst, are coupled with psychological drives like curiosity, ambition, and the desire for acceptance by one's peers. Developing a taste or forming a habit does not involve the creation of a new desire. Our natural desires are warped and twisted by repeated and evil satisfaction.

It now can be clearly seen why so-called evil desires cannot be destroyed. Because they are actually misused *normal* desires, they cannot be removed without dehumanizing us. What must happen is the correction of their misuse.

Our difficulty is intensified by the fact that sin's abuse of our desires results in *compulsive behavior.* We find ourselves enslaved by certain habits. An appetite becomes a craving that demands satisfaction. We naturally think of *addictive* habits such as the use of alcohol, tobacco, or drugs. There is a fine line that is hard to find between physical and psychological addiction. The use of alcohol—probably the most dangerous drug in our society—to the point of alcoholism can be caused by a physical demand (body chemistry) or psychological pressures, or both. The habitual use of tobacco even when its harmful effects are well known, is due more to habit patterns of behavior and stress than to physiological craving. Sadly, the myth that smoking calms the nerves is still widely believed. When I was in divinity school, an elderly physician who had spent a lifetime studying the effects of nicotine on the human body told us: "Smoking only relieves a condition it has previously created." This was many years before scientific research had substantiated the claim.

Several modern drugs and narcotics that were developed to give merciful relief and healing to those with serious illness are being tragically misused today. Our so-called drug culture is one of the ghastly scandals of our civilized world. Tragically, it has been inflamed by money-crazed and conscienceless pushers. What a vivid example of how sin takes something that is potentially redemptive and turns it into a demonic force! The spread of drug addiction is a frightening harbinger of a collapsing civilization. Almost inevitably the tragedy begins with an exhilarating experiment, usually under peer pressure, but continued use results in a degenerating total dependency.

But addiction in our society is not limited to alcohol, nicotine, and drugs. It is easy to view such substances as tragically evil and fail to see the fundamental scriptural principle: "All things are lawful for me, but I will not be mastered by anything" (1 Cor. 6:12). *Anything* that makes me its slave has stolen my freedom in Christ—no matter how much I enjoy it! Is not the person who *must* have his morning coffee at least enslaved if not addicted—particularly as medical evidence accumulates, linking "too much" (however much that is) coffee with several serious physical disorders? Of course there is a devastating difference between the nature and results of "hard addiction" (alcohol, nicotine, drugs) and bondage to coffee. But is there any difference in *principle* between such "hard addiction" and a dependency on caffeine? Does this not become a spiritual issue? When the doctor orders the total elimination of caffeine—in coffee, tea, and even soft drinks—after a heart attack or even the suspicion of one, does that not require our serious consideration, especially if we are addicted—even to cola? Perhaps we haven't realized it, but if addiction is an evidence of sin's abuse of our desires, should we not include *all* addiction?

Yet all compulsive behavior cannot be properly called addiction. Perhaps we can better understand it as *weakness.* A normal appetite, lashed by sin, becomes a grim craving—even for what we know is wrong. Although we realize that many a person's grave was "dug with his teeth," we too often compulsively overeat. As Christians we need to be more sensitive to the sin of obesity, which had a prominent place on most of the vice lists of the Early Church. It is certainly unjust to classify all overweight as obesity. Without a doubt glandular problems and an unbalanced metabolism can have a decisive effect on a person's weight. Still it is amazing how often one with weight problems simply eats too much.

The *quality* of food is fully as important as *quantity* for maintaining good health. In this day of frantic commercialization and competition, food processing has alarming and harmful amounts of preservatives and additives. Medical studies increasingly reaffirm the dangerous, and sometimes disastrous, consequences of excessive salt, sugar, or chocolate in our diet (just to name a few things). Nevertheless, how often do we indulge our special craving, even for "junk food"? During the Cuban missile crisis in 1962, when President John Kennedy and Premier Nikita Khrushchev were testing each other's moral courage, I visited with Mrs. Thompson. She openly confessed the fear we all felt. Then she showed me her well-stocked bomb cellar. In a prominent place was a five-pound box of chocolates. When I noticed them she declared, without too much embarrassment, "I have decided that if I must die, I will at least die happy."

Should we not, as Christians, be concerned about harmful eating habits? We don't always realize it, but often overindulgence is a skeleton from former years in sin when our only concern was to satisfy or even satiate ourselves. Should the excuse "It is one of my pet sins" or "I'm just not disciplined" salve our conscience? So often sin besieges our will so that what God intends to be iron becomes rubber. We have no backbone! Sin leaves behind few casualties so devastating as a deteriorated will.[1]

Fortunately, today there appears to be an increasing concern about the *spiritual* implications of improper and unhealthy eating habits. It is to be hoped that this is more than a spin-off of the present widespread obsession with physical fitness. The oft-repeated concern that our bodies are the temple of God *should include our eating habits* as well as the use of tobacco and alcohol. I vividly remember the consternation on Jim's face. As a newly born believer, he asked in a public question-and-answer session, "What should I say in answer to a fellow worker who asked: 'How can people who are fat say that smoking and drinking are wrong?'"

Certainly the questions that have been raised about eating and drinking habits have not been intended to *create* guilt. One of the prime motivations of this study has been the desire to bring *release* from unnecessary guilt. Hopefully, a realization that many of our struggles with desire in this area are directly related to "what sin leaves behind" will produce encouragement and determination to find deliverance.

Sin also wreaks havoc with our nonphysical or psychological drives. We are created with the basic emotion of fear. The proper use of it enables us to avoid physical danger and is associated with awe, or the proper fear of God. In a life lived with little or no thought of God and with total self-dependence, we develop an intense reaction to a threat against our safety, our status, or our pride. Such fear turns to terror in certain menacing situations. After we find new life in Christ, we very likely will automatically react in a habit pattern of fright when confronted with similar situations. This can become a critical arena of spiritual struggle, especially if such biblical phrases as "perfect love casts out fear" (1 John 4:18) are misinterpreted.[2]

Similarly, our natural drive of ambition is often abused by sin. While such a desire can be the springboard for worthwhile attainment, when perverted it can become an evil determination to reach the top at any cost. We must excel regardless! Again, as a new man in Christ, this impulsive habit pattern can remain. For such a person, it is difficult to experience the total dependence on Christ that must develop. Many a sincere soul struggles with this sin-abused desire.

I have made no attempt to be exhaustive, only to offer some concrete examples of the nature of the hidden struggle with desires that many experience. When we are striving to live a holy life, this hidden struggle can be a decisive and distressing battleground. We must not miss the *principles* that the Scriptures provide for us. Such things as drinking and smoking should not be legalistically categorized as evil while we ignore other vital areas of sin-abused desires. As we open our hearts, the Holy Spirit will make specific applications for us *where* we struggle.

19
Deliverance from the Old

As we observed earlier (cf. chap. 2), our problems with human frailty are not dealt with *explicitly* by name in the New Testament. However, there is *implicit* instruction for us, related to this vital concern.

> I urge you therefore, brethren, by the mercies of God, to present your bodies a living and holy sacrifice, acceptable to God, which is your spiritual service of worship. And do not be conformed to this world, but be transformed by the renewing of your mind, that you may prove what the will of God is, that which is good and acceptable and perfect *(Rom. 12:1-2).*

Paul gave us here two important emphases. When the consecration Paul pleads for occurs, and we present our bodies to God, some wonderful things begin to happen as we walk by the Spirit. First the negative—"do not be conformed," followed by the positive—"but be transformed." These essential principles have a wide range of spiritual significance but can beautifully apply to our considerations in this study (cf. chaps. 14—15).

As we live and walk by the Spirit, which total "presentation" makes possible, we find deliverance from the old grip of sin on our desires. In spite of the dissipation that years in sin develop, God has promised and provided power to set us free! Paul exhorted the Colossians: "Put to death therefore what is earthly in you . . . passion *[pathos]*, evil desire *[epithumian kakēn]*"[1] (Col. 3:5, RSV). Wouldn't it be terribly tragic if that were impossible? But, thank God, it *is* possible! Paul promised: "But I say, walk by the Spirit, and *you will not carry out the desire of the flesh*" (Gal. 5:16, italics added). There is no place where my favorite verse in the Bible (not an easy choice for a New Testament teacher to make) is a more glorious reality.

> No temptation has overtaken you but such as is common to man; and God is faithful, who will not allow you to be tempted beyond what you are able, but with the temptation will provide the way of escape also, that you may be able to endure it *(1 Cor. 10:13).*[2]

God has *guaranteed* that we will not be left with misused desires that render us helpless against sin. God says, "I won't let it happen!" Even so, the promise is not always as we expect and would prefer. Sometimes the deliverance comes as a sudden, miraculous touch, an act of healing mercy. Just as God can, and at times does, heal a physical infirmity as dramatic and spectacular as cancer, so He on occasion heals a sin-dissipated desire. We generally associate such healings with addiction to alcohol, tobacco, or other drugs. But it could be equally true of *any* addiction or weakness that is "beyond what [we] are able" to overcome. Thank God, He *is able* to heal today—instantly and completely—and at times He does.[3]

However, this does not always happen. Looking back over more than 40 years of ministry as a pastor, teacher, and evangelist, I must candidly make the admission that for everyone I saw instantly delivered from an addictive habit, there have been at least a half dozen who found deliverance only through discipline. Sometimes this involved an extended and painful struggle. Such a battle is equally true with weakness rooted in misused desires that cannot be properly called addiction. Through it all God was true to His promise.

They could and did overcome! They were not left with more than they could bear by His grace.

We naturally want to know "Why?" Why are some instantly delivered while others are left to master their sin-warped desires by painful discipline? We must be cautious here, lest a careless statement cause misunderstanding and cruel harm. We cannot presume to know fully the reasons why God does or does not act in a certain way. Howbeit, it seems He does, at times, heal instantly, both physically and psychologically, for a *specific reason.* In His infinite wisdom He knows when, in addition to all else we face, an addictive habit or weakness would be more than we could handle. It would be overwhelming.

Perhaps a hypothetical illustration might help us to understand our question better. Let's imagine that two young mothers, Mary and Betty, find new life in Christ on a Sunday evening. They are very good friends and keep in close touch with each other. They also are both heavily addicted to smoking and realize that the habit should be broken.[4] On Monday morning after the children are off to school, they are having their daily visit on the telephone. Together they are rejoicing about the wonders of their newfound salvation. Then Mary "drops the bomb." She jubilantly shares that she has not had a single desire for a cigarette since she was at the altar the night before. The habit has been suddenly taken away!

Betty is left in total bewilderment and confusion—and guilt. She is shocked because she is having the battle of her life with smoking. Always before, after the children are in bed, she would drop into her recliner in front of the TV, light up a cigarette, and relax. Last night she had a terrible struggle but somehow managed to resist the craving to smoke. It had also been a daily routine, when she was talking to Mary in the morning, to pour a cup of coffee and enjoy a cigarette. This morning the desire has been almost overpowering, but by grit and determination, praying almost constantly, she has "ached" it out. Already, in a few short hours, she has consumed an unbelievable amount of gum and candy drops, keeping something in her mouth almost every waking moment. Now Mary is saying that she has lost all desire to smoke.

Why the difference? At least part of the answer may be that Mary is married to a most difficult mate. He is doing everything possible to discourage and defeat his wife in her newfound faith, ridiculing her and putting every imaginable stumbling block in her way. God knows that if Mary had to struggle with a cigarette habit while living with such a tyrant, she just could not make it. So He lovingly reached down and healed her—instantly!

In contrast, Betty lives with an angel in human form. He is doing everything possible to assist and advance her new way of life. He will be a strong support to her. God also knows this! If she overcomes her tobacco habit learning to lean heavily on Him and His grace, she will have a stronger faith and a greater capacity for discipline in the days ahead.

No matter what the compulsive desires might be, even addiction or intense weakness, *we can be sure of sufficient grace to overcome.* God has guaranteed victory! "I won't let you be overwhelmed. You will not be left with more than you can overcome by My grace." If we are left to struggle with a habit or weakness—*of any kind*—we *can* overcome it by discipline.

The secret is "learning to lean." We can't do it in our own strength—we will fail. As we walk by His Spirit, trusting in Him, we discover His strength and power. But we must be diligent to pray and depend upon Him. It is not a matter of breathing a prayer and then expecting a miracle! Instead, we must live moment by moment in intimate fellowship with Him.

Learning to lean, learning to lean,
I'm learning to lean on Jesus.
Finding more power than I'd ever dreamed,
I'm learning to lean on Jesus.
—JOHN STALLINGS*

But the sad truth is that all too often the "Marys," who have been instantly healed, tell the "Bettys," who are struggling with a habit or weakness, that their problem persists because they have not "paid the price" or "exercised enough faith." *They make their experience of healing normative,* and insist that if Betty would only "die out," she could have instant victory.

Many years ago while pastoring in Greater Boston, I witnessed God's guaranteed victory dramatic in a experience. Jane, a lovely young lady in her 20s and a nurse at the local hospital, was converted in our church. She surprised me with the news a short time later that she was admitting herself to the hospital. When I asked the reason, she explained that some time previously her doctor had inadvertently allowed her to become addicted to morphine following major surgery. Since then she had been maintaining her addiction from the hospital supply of narcotics. Now, with her new faith, she realized that this was wrong and was determined to find deliverance. When she entered the hospital, I started a daily vigil of visitation and prayer.

Jane was an unusually neat and attractive young woman. She dressed immaculately and there was never a hair out of place. After a few days the sides of her hospital bed were raised. Increasingly she looked more like a caged animal than the Jane I knew. Her hair was disheveled and her face was so badly scratched that the nurses had to tie her arms to the bed. Each day her eyes sunk deeper into her head. She was suffering the indescribable agonies of withdrawal from an addiction.

Then one day she looked up at me from her prison of torment and declared, "I am giving up. I thought I could make it, but I can't. I must call for relief." Then, without a thought, I spontaneously leaned over the bed rail and asked, "Jane, don't you realize what God has promised you?" And I quoted 1 Cor. 10:13. (I imagine that I probably used this favorite verse in visitation—especially in the hospital—almost more than the rest of the Bible put together.) Strongly I emphasized "God will not allow . . . beyond what you are able." Her haunting eyes suddenly began to glow as she asked, "Do you mean *that* is for me, in this condition?"

Then it seemed that Satan jumped on my left shoulder and hissed in my ear, "You unscrupulous scoundrel, how could you hold out a straw to a person in such a desperate condition?" But immediately Someone else was on my right shoulder, whispering: "But son, it is true!" I leaned back over the bed and said with a smile, "Jane, if I ever believed anything in my life, I believe that promise is for you—now!"

I don't know how she did it, but she managed to wiggle her hand free enough to sink her fingernails into my wrist until the blood came. Her eyes sparkled as she asserted, "I can make it now." And make it she did! Not too many days later Jane walked out of that hospital—a free woman, all by naked faith in God's guarantee: "I won't leave you with more than you can overcome by My grace."

There *is* deliverance from the addiction and weakness that sin wreaks on our desires. It is not always—not even often—in a sudden dramatic healing. But as certainly as there is a God in heaven and on earth, as we learn to lean on Him, there is grace for total victory—always and for everyone!

20
Discovering the New

It is important to remember that the negative is *never* the end! (Cf. chap 15.) We must find deliverance from the old and evil ways of fulfilling our desires. But that must never be our final objective. If it is, we miss much that Paul and the entire New Testament teach about the promises of God.

Paul exhorted (Rom. 12:2) not only to "be not conformed," but also to "be transformed" (cf. chap. 15). By the Holy Spirit, we are to discover the proper and right satisfaction of our desires. New habit patterns of fulfillment must be created. This is an essential part of the transformation that the new man in Christ undergoes as he walks by the Spirit. How beautifully Paul described it:

> But we all, with unveiled face beholding as in a mirror the glory of the Lord, are being transformed into the same image from glory to glory, just as from the Lord, the Spirit *(2 Cor. 3:18)*.

Too often it is forgotten that every desire we have was placed there by God! There is a right and holy purpose for each one. That is why they are within us. We can discover that purpose by the Holy Spirit. From a new and holy heart, no longer in the grip of self-centeredness, God will teach us by the Holy Spirit. As we are taught, a remarkable truth emerges. Very often in the discovery of the new we are finally and totally delivered from the old! The new displaces the old. When I was in college preparing for the ministry, we studied a homiletical masterpiece by Thomas Chalmers titled "The Expulsive Power of a New Affection." The sermon contained a spiritual principle of prime importance. As we are captured by the new, the grip of the old is broken. New and holy satisfaction of our desires will cause the old and evil embrace to let loose.

We all have strong desires of hunger and thirst. These appetites have no moral sensitivity. Our stomach does not know if the food we are enjoying was obtained by our honest toil—or stolen. So the gratification of these desires can be easily misdirected. As suggested in an earlier chapter (18), we often develop a compulsive desire for too much, or harmful, food and drink. This obsession can be overcome as we learn to enjoy the eating and drinking that will produce good health. It is not enough—in fact is often counterproductive— merely to *seek to abstain from* our harmful dietary enjoyments. To tell ourselves, "We can't" or "We shouldn't," will simply focus our attention psychologically on the forbidden. Instead, the discovery of a new and proper satisfaction of those basic appetites will result in the former avenues of indulgence fading into insignificance.

Unfortunately, many spiritually minded people treat the subject of sex in an abnormal and often destructive manner. This undoubtedly stems from our society's corruption of human sexuality and our fear of its power over us. The result of this hush-hush attitude has often been a disastrous lack of sex education. Even worse, well-meaning parents, in a desperate attempt to protect their children from our sex-saturated society, sometimes leave them with a tragic aversion to sex. For them, sex is something unclean and to be avoided at all costs. Many pastors and marital counselors find this to be a root cause of conflict between husbands and wives. While some of the modern-day attempts at sex education are grossly indecent and foolishly idealistic,[1] there is a crying need for sound Christian teaching. A proper limit exists as to what can be presented in public, especially in mixed groups, both in school and church. But there is no excuse for parents to fail to meet this vital need in their homes. It is sad indeed for a child to have to learn about sex from his peers.

Though God put our sex drive in us, we may well ask, What is its purpose? Although it brings supernal and exhilarating pleasure, that is not its primary God-given intent. Those who suggest that it is are hedonistic, finding in pleasure life's highest good. Neither did God create sex for the *primary* reason of procreation. That surely is one of its proper functions, but some people cannot have children. Does that mean they cannot experience the true purpose of sex? Certainly not! Jesus himself spoke of the highest fulfillment of sex:

> "But from the beginning of creation, God MADE THEM MALE AND FEMALE. FOR THIS CAUSE A MAN SHALL LEAVE HIS FATHER AND MOTHER, AND THE TWO SHALL BECOME ONE FLESH; consequently they are no longer two, but one flesh. What therefore God has joined together, let no man separate" (*Mark 10:6-9*).

This goes all the way back to Adam (cf. Gen. 2:24). It is only sexual intercourse that can take a man and woman and make them "one flesh." God created sex *primarily* for this high and noble purpose. For this reason, when it is thus observed, we discover one of life's most beautiful experiences. It is what might be called a *human* sacrament. This is why sex outside of marriage is a shameful sacrilege. Increasingly, the flood tide of our modern "sex liberation" makes such a standard appear as a hopeless ideal. It seems as ridiculous as trying to repair a crumbling dike with a plaster patch. In spite of this trend, however, there can be no doubt whatever about the clear teaching of the Scriptures. Further, the true purpose of sex gives us the strongest biblical argument against the most tragic blight of this sexual revolution—homosexuality. No matter how it is stated, the homosexual is saying, "I find more pleasure with my own sex." That is hedonism!

Unfortunately, because of abuse, the true purpose and fulfillment of sex is difficult to find. When it has been promiscuously practiced, partners in marriage are often defrauded of the extraphysical or "spiritual" pleasure of a conjugal relationship. This needs to be stressed along with the moral and physical consequences of extramarital sexual activity. Few things are more satisfying and beautiful than to begin this very precious relationship on one's wedding night. Sad to say, with the tragic harvest of our modern movement toward free love—with conservative statistics revealing sexual activity among more than 50 percent of our teenage young people, not to mention illicit relationships among college students and the shameful example of their parents—there is little hope of realizing this goal. A wedding is rare when both bride and groom are chaste! This has made a hollow mockery of the beautiful symbolism of the white wedding gown.

Without the wondrous redemptive power of the gospel, how easy it is to be cynical. In spite of the misuse of this God-given drive, by the Holy Spirit we *can* learn the true meaning of sex in our marriages. Thus there can be an increasing healing of this perverted desire.

We spoke also of how sin leaves behind skeletons from the serious misuse of our natural emotion of fear (chap. 18). The manifestations of this obsession vary from stark terror to quiet timidity. Sometimes it is hidden, but often it is vividly seen. How can the trauma that results be overcome? Certainly there must be more than the insistent telling of ourselves, "I must not be afraid." Even the logical question, "What is there to be afraid of?" does not dispel fear. Total deliverance from fear can only come as we, by the Holy Spirit, *learn* the true reason for this instinct. In the simplest sense, fear has been given to us as a means of self-preservation. Just as our bloodstream rushes defensive aids to an area that is attacked by infection, so we spontaneously react in fear when we are conscious that our safety is threatened. This is nothing to be ashamed of. Unfortunately, there are those who attempt to convince others that they are unafraid of danger. Fearlessness is often vaunted as a virtue, when many times such a person is trying most to convince himself. Often such so-called fearlessness has proved to be foolishness. We ought to be afraid of danger! On the battlefield many a soldier has performed monumental deeds of courage while gripped with fear.

Because of sin's abuse, sad to say, we can be afraid of our own shadow! A senseless fear is certainly unhealthy. From the pulpit I have often tried to make a crucial distinction which is more than a play on words. We all need to *have* fears (and concerns), but we must not allow them to *have us!* There is a big difference. If after a life in sin, we discover that our fears still "have us," what should we do? As urged in the last chapter, we must find deliverance as we learn to lean on the Holy Spirit. But beyond that we will find total freedom from destructive fear only as the Holy Spirit teaches us the greatest purpose of fear. It is so true that we need to leave our fears with Him, but in addition He will patiently make plain that the highest expression of fear is when it is directed toward our eternal welfare. Only then can we fear sin, as we ought, and its death-rendering effects.

In the next section we will be dealing with anger as it is expressed in our lives. Therefore we will not treat it here, except to make one basic observation. The emotion of anger was given to us by God and is not *intrinsically* evil. Often the Bible speaks of God's anger or wrath and even of Jesus being angry.[2] Also, human anger is even commanded. "BE ANGRY, AND yet DO NOT SIN" (Eph. 4:26). But the verse includes this vital caution: "Do not let the sun go down on your anger." Anger was given to us to incite us to action against sin and injustice. It is psychological adrenalin! Sadly, though, it has been misused to defend an offended self.

Another basic human instinct which has caused people a lot of trouble (cf. Eve in the Garden of Eden, Genesis 3) is curiosity. Certainly one of its primary purposes is to inspire us to search for the good, the right, and the holy—but not the forbidden. Curiosity is often a prime motivation for study and learning. Where better than in searching God's Word and finding His will?

There is in each of us, in varying degrees, a love of beauty. Again, in our sin-distorted society, men have prostituted this lovely instinct. Too often that which is vulgar and sexually suggestive is displayed as something beautiful. An oft heard excuse is "Beauty is in the eye of the beholder." However, true beauty *always* points beyond the object to the Artist from whom all genuine beauty flows. It can be beauty in nature—a breathtaking sunrise or sunset or a mountain ablaze with a multicolored coat; or in human beings—with striking physical features or a love-exuding personality. But if it is true beauty, it will reflect the Maker of it all. The Holy Spirit is eager to show us true beauty.

Another human drive, already discussed in chapter 18, is ambition. How often the new man in Christ is left with a residue of inordinate or misdirected ambition. Years of self-centered living pervert and distort this God-given trait. There is nothing wrong with the desire to excel. What is needed is a new orientation. Now that he has a new center of reference —God's will rather than self-gratification—the newborn believer has "one deep, supreme desire . . . to be like Jesus."* This becomes the greatest ambition of his life, to please God. Every desire to excel, *even in spiritual things,* must be fashioned to God's will. The faithful ministry of the Holy Spirit

---

*Thomas O. Chisholm, "I Want to Be Like Jesus." Copyright 1945. Renewed 1973 by Lillenas Publishing Co.

teaches us increasingly what such total commitment involves. So often we say that the follower of Christ should put first things first. But before that is possible, *he must learn what is first.* This involves the developing of a whole new set of values and priorities. Significantly, Paul's prayer for his beloved Philippians includes: "that you may approve the things that are excellent" (Phil. 1:10). This petition is literally translated: "that you might distinguish the differing." This speaks of a new sense of values. But to pursue this involves a spiritual quest in which we increasingly discover the fullest realization of our highest ambition.

Once more, differing from person to person is the desire for friendship. A more technical term is *gregariousness.* Often the devil's last chain that gallingly binds us capitalizes on our human desire to be accepted. Over and over he uses the refrain: "If you give your life to God you will lose all your friends." What a colossal and hellish lie! The truth is just the opposite. When we find Christ, we receive a new family. We don't become believers in isolation. Instead, we are members of the Body of Christ. A holy bond blends us together as a family. In true fellowship there is self-giving. How different from a world where the primary concern is "looking out for number one." In its place, we are concerned to be "our brother's brother." Nowhere else on earth can there be such belonging. "Blest be the tie that binds our hearts in Christian love" (John Fawcett).

There has been opportunity here only to give some suggestions as to *how* the Holy Spirit would teach us to discover the new and right fulfillment of our desires. He must make the specific application to each of us. This is the pathway to the re-creation of misused desires.

21
Watch Out!

As we search, with the leadership of the Holy Spirit, for the right fulfillment of our desires, we must be cautious about a couple of dangerous areas. There have always been those who have confused a holy life with being eccentric or peculiar. It is true that a Christian is different from the world in which he lives, a world that has no time or thought of God.[1] But that "difference" does not consist of strange and bizarre behavior. Some in the holiness movement have appeared to be proud of their eccentric dress and conduct. Perhaps this is due, at least in part, to the KJV translation of Titus 2:14: "Who gave himself for us, that he might redeem us from all iniquity, and purify unto himself a *peculiar* people, zealous of good works" (italics added). In the 17th century (when the KJV was translated), "peculiar" did not mean what it does today. This is the only place in the New Testament where this Greek term (*periousios*) is used, and thus it is difficult to be certain of its exact meaning. It carries the idea of "chosen" or "special,"[2] as is reflected in modern translations.[3] To be God's "chosen" or "special" ones *will* make us different! But this does not mean that we are peculiar or odd. When we are "odd"—then we simply are "odd"! There are a lot of odd or peculiar people who aren't very holy.

It is psychologically dangerous to make unnecessary or abnormal restrictions on our desires and emotions. There is not only a *right,* but also a *normal* fulfillment for every one. It is this that the Holy Spirit wants to teach us. That is why asceticism (cf. chap. 14) can never produce the holy life that God designs for us. Too often it is forgotten that *it is sin that causes abnormal living.*

Another place where we must be cautious is in the awareness that God has given us a vital responsibility. He expects us to be wise enough not to knowingly, let alone intentionally, put ourselves into situations that provoke temptation. During 15 years of college teaching, with a large freshman class every fall and spring, I repeatedly emphasized this. But it is a truth that applies to all of us regardless of our age.

For 13 years I taught at Bethany Nazarene College. The city of Bethany, Okla., is located between two lakes, Hefner to the northeast and Overholser to the southwest. At least in my earliest years, Lake Overholser was a favorite "lover's haunt" for the college students. I had not been there long before I began referring to it as Lake "Holdhercloser." With a twinkle in my eye, yet with dead earnestness, I would remind my beloved freshman "kids": "I don't care how holy you are. You can't lay in someone's arms in the backseat of a car at Lake 'Holdhercloser' and then fold your hands piously and pray: 'Now, Lord, please lead me.'" That is sheer nonsense! God expects us to have more sense. We have the responsibility of not putting ourselves into compromising situations that invite deep temptation.

Perhaps it sounds a bit silly, but we would be surprised to know how many Satan has tripped up with this argument. He encourages us to *prove* how strong we are, in the very points where we have been weak. Never will I forget an experience I had many years ago. For months I had prayed and supported a man in middle life as he sought and finally found deliverance from a lifelong tobacco habit. Then one day I was shocked to see a box of expensive cigars on his dresser, and so I asked him, "Why in the world are those cigars there?"

With a smile he answered, "I am so glad to be free from that miserable habit that I just want to show the devil how strong I am."

Forcibly, but I trust not unlovingly, I replied, "The devil is making a fool out of you." He laughed at my concern. But before very many weeks had gone by, in a weak moment he was smoking a cigar almost before he knew it. I could almost see the sly grin on the devil's face.

No matter what our area of struggle and difficulty might have been with misused desires, we should shun it like the plague. Perhaps some would disagree with me, but I don't think God would ask a converted alcoholic to go into a bar and witness to the bartender. I think He has more sense!

PART VI—IMPULSIVE BEHAVIOR DISCIPLINED

It is true that sometimes our "heart action" is faulty, reflecting the weakness of our human house. We have been so abused by sin that what we *purpose* in our hearts and even *attempt* to do is imperfectly produced. The sensitive soul constantly seeks to more perfectly express outwardly in his life what he is experiencing inwardly in his heart. Every honest person, realizing his own failures in this area, will have compassion for others.

We do believe that God sees our hearts and knows our purposes. He also understands our weaknesses that stem from both natural constitution and sinful living. Still, we *are* morally responsible for *voluntary* activity. Sadly, for some, so many so-called shortcomings are considered acquitted by God's love that license and even indulgence are justified. *God does not excuse or ignore willful transgressions.* The activity that comes from our hearts *should* mirror what God has done and is doing in our lives (cf. chap. 11). Voluntary transgression is sin and should be treated as such! Thank God, there is forgiveness and restoration—on both the vertical and horizontal planes, with God and men. "My little children, I am writing these things to you that you may not sin. And if anyone sins, we have an Advocate with the Father, Jesus Christ the righteous" (1 John 2:1).

The longer we have lived in sin, the more scarred will be our "vessel," and the more intense will be the struggle. But God has promised sufficient grace for everyone (2 Cor. 12:9). Most of us have had to make use of God's gracious provisions—perhaps many times.

But our basic concern in this study is in another sphere. We must battle with misused desires after we experience salvation. As we seek to live a holy life, we often find another sphere of spiritual struggle—and too many times defeat. It is in the activity—words spoken and deeds done—that does *not* come from the heart. Instead, such is impulsive behavior that reflects our basic temperament, our disposition, and the habits of earlier years. When we are confronted with a stimulus in our environment, we *react,* often without thinking, in accordance with our personality.

Too often this involuntary activity is unchristlike and contrary to love. In fact, it does not *at all* reflect what is in our heart. Still, we are grieved—or should be! Many times we are filled with condemnation and guilt. Are we doomed to a life of dismal failure here? Is there any hope of victorious living—at the impulsive level? To this we now turn.

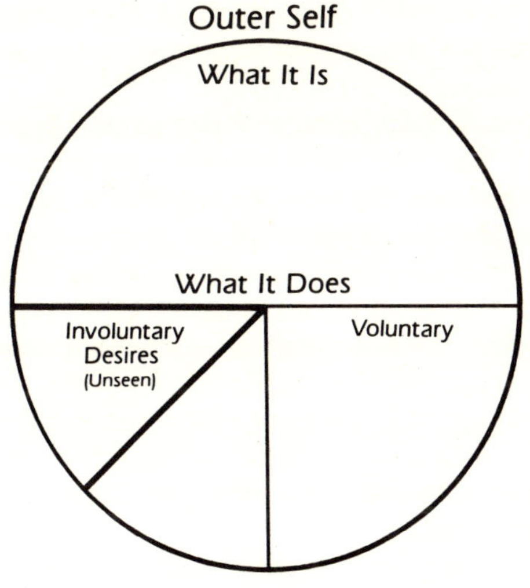

Outer Self
What It Is
What It Does
Involuntary
Desires
(Unseen)
Voluntary

22
Personality Quirks

Perhaps we don't realize it, because usually we are the last ones to see them, but we all have idiosyncrasies that are really quirks. We might want to deny that they exist, but those who live close to us know all about them. They are a vital part of our personality. How—and why—does this happen?

First, we must remember that the same influences which formed our old inner personhood also shaped our outer personality (cf. chap. 9).[1] Because the outer self was the only avenue of expression of the old inner self, the outer took on the character of the inner.

At the same time the *nature* of that old inner self should be kept in mind. We saw (chap. 9) what sin did to us within. There was not only inborn depravity, which we identified as self-sovereignty, but also the evil attitudes that resulted from continuous indulgence of self-centeredness. As our sinful hearts manifested themselves in our lives, a distinctive personality developed. There were behavioral tendencies, dispositional characteristics, and temperament traits. Most significantly, for our study, habit patterns of impulsive response to the stimuli of our environment were formed.

Furthermore, in chapter 11 it was pointed out that salvation basically deals with the inner self. God gives us a new heart, and He becomes our new Lord. Notwithstanding, this new inner self can only be expressed through an old outer self. Our new heart can only be seen through our old body—even more specifically, through our personality. When we lived in sin, with little or no thought of pleasing God or acting out of love, habit patterns of behavior were built up and deeply grooved in us.

Of course, this conduct that is contrary to Christian love is erratic or spasmodic. We hope it is not constant! But at times it *does* appear. Its specific form differs greatly with the individual. Some are moody and so uncommunicative, for no apparent reason, that we are left with the question, "What have I done?" Some are so sensitive that even a look, to say nothing of a word, causes an offense. Some are so fussy and picky that nothing is ever done right. Some are so stubborn that nothing can change their minds. Some are always critical and faultfinding of everyone. Some insist on meddling in everyone else's business. So—— The list could go on endlessly. We will have to make our own specific applications regarding ourselves.

What makes this such a crucial problem is that these personality manifestations are often impulsive. They do not come from the heart but are involuntary reactions. We can have the holiest of hearts and the best possible intentions, and yet leave the wrong impression. We are misunderstood and poorly express what is in our hearts. As a result we hurt our witness for Christ. If we are at all spiritually sensitive, we grieve over our behavior and often go on a guilt trip.

What we *must* see, in ourselves and others, is that there is a vital distinction to be made. Did what we say or do come from our hearts? Or was it impulsive behavior, patterned on our personality—perhaps a quirk? The difference *is* important!

23
The Big Bugaboo

We purposely did not mention one impulsive personality expression because it needs special consideration. Without a doubt the most common involuntary reaction that we have is *anger.* We impulsively follow the habit pattern of an involuntary indignant word or act—*as a reaction.* Sometimes we snap at our wife or husband, we shout at the children, or we are quick with a friend. If you do not have this problem, you should be on your knees every day thanking God—so many do!

A story is told of one of our early general superintendents. (The story may be apocryphal; I question whether it actually happened, but in any case it makes a good illustration.) During a district assembly an elderly pastor was giving his report. He evidently had not accomplished very much the past year becase he went to great lengths telling of his wonderful marriage. He finished with the decisive statement: "In over 50 years of marriage, I don't remember wife and me ever having an angry moment." When he sat down, the general superintendent, who had shown unusual patience, looked at the pastor and declared, "My dear brother, either you have a bad memory, or you are a liar."

When we speak of anger, we must be sure that we know what is meant. We are not talking about willful wrath (*thumos*), which is hardly impulsive.[1] In many ways, the violence of *thumos* is temporary insanity, as illustrated by the riot at Ephesus (Acts 19:28). It can have no place in the life of a newborn child of God. Instead, we mean by anger that indignation that was used for years to pamper and protect a sinful heart. Often such indignation is involuntarily expressed after we find salvation.

It is a strange mystery why this personality problem has been marked by many in the holiness movement as the certain sign of a sinful heart. The illustrations are legion of "carnal fits"—kicking the cow, throwing the cat, or beating the horse (or sometimes the wife). To some, the supreme evidence that they are sanctified is that under any and all provocations, they have a calm and unperturbed spirit—even when the clothesline breaks and the clean clothes fall in the mud. Tragically, there is not even remote scriptural support for such an idea!

What we need to see is that angry reactions are *personality problems* (quirks), just like several other things (cf. chap. 22). How well I remember, many years ago, when a professor from Eastern Nazarene College spoke to our Greater Boston preachers' gathering. We were wrestling with this question of holy living and human failures. He shocked us when he declared, "I have never been angry in my life—before I was saved, before I was sanctified, or since." Seeing our look of amazement, he quickly went on to add, "But I have some other problems!"

It is of greatest importance for us to realize that involuntary anger is but one of many personality problems. For the purpose of illustration, I am going to imagine some members of a church board with whom a pastor might have to contend. If the characterizations sound extreme, it is a matter of exaggeration for emphasis. Sister White is so sensitive, wearing her feelings on her sleeve, that the pastor has to walk an almost impossible tightrope to keep from hurting or offending her. Brother Brown is so stubborn that once he has formed an opinion, even the Lord himself couldn't change his mind. Brother Green is so pugnacious or argumentative that he is always "agin it," no matter what it is. (Of course, the wise pastor knows how to plant the idea in the board member's mind beforehand so that he thinks it is his idea.) Sister Black is constantly critical and finds fault with everyone and everything. All of these personality quirks—sensitivity, stubbornness, pugnaciousness, and faultfinding—are viewed as unfortunate. However, if they are expressed calmly and under control, everyone agrees that they are only human weaknesses. On the other hand, if on occasion Brother Purple blows his top in evident anger, we assume that he is sinful and needs to get sanctified!

Sadly, we fail many times to see that *all* spontaneous reactions, *including anger,* are psychologically the same thing. They are impulsive personality responses! There is no valid basis whatever to pick out one—anger—and label it sinful, while excusing all the others as human weakness. If one is sinful, they all are! If one is human weakness, they all are! So often the unfortunate soul who gets angry is hounded by guilt and can envision help only as a sudden deliverance. This seldom comes, and he either lives a life of agonizing despair or drops out as a spiritual casualty. After more than 40 years of ministry, I look back at the number with this problem whom I failed to help. It is not a pleasant memory! At the same time the others, feeling justified because of their weakness, do nothing about their problem and live out their lives severely crippled by their warped personalities.

24
God's Guarantee

It is not enough simply to identify the problem and even commiserate about it. What can be done about all the personality problems or quirks? Are we imprisoned in an old human house where we can expect nothing but despair and defeat? Can God do anything for us in the area of personality problems? Let us thank Him that He can and will!

As we live and walk by the Spirit—and only then—these habit patterns of personality can be broken through His discipline. Undoubtedly there are more, but the glorious promise of Rom. 8:13 has a special application to the old habit patterns that sin leaves behind.

> For if you are living according to the flesh, you must die; but if by the Spirit you are putting to death the *deeds* of the body, you will live *(italics added)*.

The word "deeds" *(praxeis)* has been called the closest word in the Greek language to what we mean by "habit patterns."[1] The picture is vivid and even dramatic. *If* we live according to (by means of) the flesh (our strength), we will die; but *if* instead we are putting to death the habit patterns of this old body by the Spirit (in His power), we shall live. It would be sadistic torment if that promise and prospect were beyond our reach. Habit patterns of impulsive personality behavior *can* be broken!

The wondrous promise of 1 Cor. 10:13, which we related to misused desires, certainly applies here. It is "God's Guarantee."

> No temptation has overtaken you but such as is common to man; and God is faithful, who will not allow you to be tempted beyond what you are able, but with the temptation will provide the way of escape also, that you may be able to endure it *(1 Cor. 10:13)*.

As we noted in chapter 19, "temptation" *(peirasmos)* includes *all* testing and trial—even due to personality weakness. Also, as with misused desires, sometimes deliverance comes in a dramatic moment when God touches us. We are healed of a perverted personality trait instantly and miraculously. Most of us have heard testimonies of such victories, especially over anger. One day the person had a mean—even vicious—and uncontrollable temper. Then, in answer to prayer, God took it away. I can believe that! I can honestly say that I have witnessed it. *But such deliverance is spiritual healing.* It is not an *intrinsic* part of either regeneration or sanctification.

As in all healing it does not happen to all who ask. The response to the prayer lies in the mystery of God's will. Oftentimes—in fact most times—victory over a perverted personality trait is gained by the gradual, and sometimes painful, discipline of the Holy Spirit. It is *only* as we learn to lean on Him moment by moment that victory comes. All too many times we struggle to get up after a disappointing failure due to our living by the flesh. Patiently the Lord strives to teach us *total* dependence on Him. But we can be sure—God guarantees it—that if we are left to struggle and discipline a personality habit pattern, we can overcome it by His grace. As certain as God is alive, we can gain the victory.

This is one crucial area of growth—learning to express more perfectly outwardly what we are experiencing inwardly. It is a matter of total commitment to His discipline. As suggested in chapter 14, there are times when we need to be "spanked." But beyond that it is necessary to keep our lives open to His disciplining touch. He is molding and shaping us into the person He wants us to be.

But just as with those who experience miraculous healing of a misused desire, the one who undergoes a sudden and total personality change is inclined to make his experience normative. He is sure that it can happen to anyone if the other person will only pay the price. This is built on the wrong premise! Any and all divine healing comes not because we have "paid a price." It is an act of mercy that God, in His infinite wisdom, wills. In chapter 19 we suggested some plausible human explanations of why healing does or does not happen. But we always stand back in wonder and acknowledge our finite understanding.

Finally, many times we are severely tried because some battles seem never to be fully won. How many times do we gain the victory in one area of impulsive behavior only then to see another glaring failure? This is many times because we are receiving new light. What once was never even seen, now becomes an issue of conscience in the glow of love's new revelation. We should not let such experiences discourage us. Instead, we need to thank God for new light. We are making progress and simply feeling the "growing pains."

25
The Expulsive Power of a New Affection

In chapter 20, while dealing with misused desires, I referred to the great sermon by Thomas Chalmers titled "The Expulsive Power of a New Affection." We saw that here is a vital spiritual principle for dealing with human desire. It is equally important as we seek to live victoriously on the battlefield of impulsive behavior.

The wise parent has learned this in dealing with his children. Constant prohibition—saying, "No," or "Don't"—psychologically focuses attention on the forbidden. If a small child appears with a sharp knife in his hand, probably the worst thing possible would be to scream, "Drop it!" More than likely the frightened child would cut himself. However, if the parent could find an attractive object—a red ball would be ideal—and hold it out to the child, what would happen? Impulsively, he would probably drop the knife and reach for the ball.

If we could only learn this basic principle in spiritual matters how much heartache and defeat we could escape! If ever the principle is valid it is so in the realm of impulsive behavior. It is not enough to break old habit patterns by the help of the Holy Spirit, as important as that is. We need to let Him build new ones into our lives.

As we live and walk by the Spirit, He will lovingly transform us, teaching us how to respond spontaneously in loving ways. When we remember what "transformation" means, the gradual metamorphosis from being the person we *were* to becoming the person He wants us to be, the journey is exciting. Patiently and persistently, He would shape and mold us so that daily we will be more like Jesus—transformed into His image (cf. 2 Cor. 3:18). Our outer personality characteristics *can be* gradually changed, sweetened, reshaped, remolded, refined, and polished.

There is only one stipulation: *It must be our deepest desire.* "My desire—to be like Jesus;/My desire—to be like Him!"* This must be more than a song that we sentimentally sing. Instead, it has to be the commitment of our lives. Increasingly I am convinced that most of us do not see more improvement in our impulsive behavior because *we don't desire it enough.* One of the most thrilling truths I know, which I never tire of sharing, is that God *wants* to do it more than we want Him to! That is the basic secret of assurance when we come to Him. How wrong it is to plead and beg, as if God is reluctant and waiting for some special evidence of our sincerity. *He wants to make us more like Jesus.* That is *His* desire. All that He asks is the opportunity. If this is *our* desire, and we demonstrate it by opening our lives as we walk with Him, God is waiting to do it.

---

*Lillian Plankenhorn, "My Desire." Copyright Fred Bock Music Co., 1946. Renewed 1974.

26
Some Practical Help

We all need some specific things to do that will help us in our struggle with impulsive behavior. My prayerful hope is that you will find practical help in some basic principles.

Check your heart. Only you and God know whether the words spoken or the deeds done came from your heart or were a spontaneous reaction. No one else can possibly know, even your closest loved ones—not even your pastor! But *you* can know if you want to. How precious is the knowledge that God knows my heart. In many dark nights of self-condemnation this has been my *only* star, but its glow enabled me to keep my bearings.

Face the facts honestly. Have enough moral courage to call your problem what it is. If it is anger, then label it that. Do you know that there are people who act hostile, disgusted, impatient, irritated, and upset, but in their own eyes they never get angry? Whom do you think they are deceiving? Don't hide it. Dig the skeleton out of the closet and face it honestly, whatever the personality quirk is. Don't forget—we all have *some.* God will show you yours *if* you want and are willing to see *it.*

See it in all its ugliness. Make yourself look at it—long and hard. See how it hurts others, how it dishonors God, how it destroys your witness. Grieve over it, not in front of the church, but alone with God. Realize that it must be changed. Let it become an issue of conscience and obedience.

Confess it to God. Perhaps you think that there is no need of a personal confession after you have experienced salvation. Maybe you associate it with a confessional or a liturgy of confession. But something vital has been lost in the nonconfessional church, where there is little, if any, formal confession as a part of worship. We don't agree theologically with the confessional churches, especially if confession is made to man. Nevertheless, we miss much if there is no place in our spiritual living for confession. Did you ever ask why confession to God is made? We certainly are not telling Him something He doesn't know. Unquestionably our confession to God is for *our benefit.* It is a vital spiritual therapy *for us.* So we need to confess to Him our failures due to impulsive behavior. It does *us* good.

Be humbled. If your involuntary word or act has hurt someone, then seek his forgiveness. Don't make it a tongue-in-cheek apology. Go to him in true humility and express how sorry you are. As you do you will make a surprising discovery. In fact you will never quite get over how much a humbling apology helps to break a habit pattern. Try it!

Visualize God's smile. A great deal has been learned today about behavior modification at the conscious level. We know that rewards for accomplishment produce a strong incentive for changed behavior. A pat on the back produces much more than a kick in the pants! Most of us have a lot to learn in this area. If this is true at the conscious level, why would it not be equally so with unconscious activity? When you have seen decisive improvement with an impulsive reaction, try to visualize the smile of God. He also rejoices in your victory. This could very well result in subconscious motivation.

Be constantly vigilant. Make your concern about your personality problems a matter of daily and earnest prayer. Remember that God *wants* to help you more than you want to be helped—right here. *And He will.* But we must be vigilant. It is not a matter of dropping on one knee, closing one eye, telling God your need, and then going on your busy way. Daily we have to throw open our lives to the power of His Spirit to *energize* us. One of God's greatest promises is this: "Now to Him who is able to do exceeding abundantly beyond all that we ask or think, *according to the power [dunamis] that works [energeō] within us*" (Eph. 3:20, italics added).[1]

The only limit to God's power (*dunamis*, spiritual dynamite) is "according to the power that *works*[2] within us." *We* determine how much we will be energized by God's mighty power. Yes, we too have a *"work" to do!* Our work is to keep our lives open to Him so that He is *able* to work.[3] The tremendous promise we have been looking at follows one of Paul's greatest prayers.

> For this reason, I bow my knees before the Father, from whom every family in heaven and on earth derives its name, that He would grant you, according to the riches of His glory, to be strengthened with power through His Spirit in the inner man; so that Christ may dwell in your hearts through faith; and that you, being rooted and grounded in love, may be able to comprehend with all the saints what is the breadth and length and height and depth, and to know the love of Christ which surpasses knowledge, that you may be filled up to all the fulness of God *(Eph. 3:14-19).*

Will not such a God as this help us with our need?

One place of special vigilance is in the area of spiritual balance. The devil has destroyed many people by getting them to carry a good thing too far. A. W. Tozer sounded this warning as well as it has ever been given. Our boldness must not become brazenness, our frankness become rudeness, our watchfulness become suspicion, our seriousness become somberness, or our conscientiousness become overscrupulousness.[4]

During the early years of the Second World War when there was much despair and fear, on their weekly Sunday evening broadcast Phil Spitalny's all-girl orchestra and choir never failed to bring inspiration with their parting words: "American patrol, with arms for the army, ships for the navy, let this be our goal, we must be vigilant, we must be vigilant."

Vigilance is the battle cry that holds the key in our spiritual warfare with our impulsive behavior.

27
The Goal Supreme

Several years ago I spent many hours with Dr. Timothy Smith, who is now professor of history and director of the program of American religious history at the Johns Hopkins University, studying and sharing our thoughts about the subject matter of this book. I am deeply indebted to him for many insights about this difficult subject. I am sure that many of my actual words and expressions can be traced to his assistance through conscious suggestions and much by unconscious influence.

One dramatic incident he shared with me came from his early pastoral experience in Greater Boston. A leading saint in his small church was dying, and he made a final pastoral call on her. At the door her daughter met him and explained that her mother had been in a deep coma for two days and had not responded to the closest members of her family. Tim was busy attending Harvard University as well as pastoring his church. The thoughtful family said there was nothing he could do for their mother. But Tim insisted that he would like to have one more prayer with her, for she had been such a blessing to him in his ministry as a young pastor.

Tim entered the sickroom, where the mother lay unconscious. Her hands and arms were on the bed covers. Kneeling by the bed, he placed one of the wrinkled hands between his, and, bending close to her ear, he began to pray. He praised

God for His wonderful grace that had saved her so many years before as a teenager. Now He had marvelously kept her for more than 60 years. In his prayer Tim blessed God for the sacrifice of His Son on the Cross and for the cleansing power of the blood of Jesus.

Then a totally unexpected thing happened! Her lips, which had been silent for over 48 hours, began to move. Those standing by heard her quietly say, "Praise God for the blood of Jesus. Amen. Bless His name." She was still unconscious! She never did regain consciousness and died in the coma.

What had happened? Her life had been so deeply disciplined as she walked and lived by the Spirit, her patterns of response so fully set by years of habitually choosing the right and the good, that now, when she could no longer hear or recognize the voices of children and loved ones, she *unconsciously* responded to prayer and praise to God. When she was past human knowing, her heart and body reacted automatically to hearing of Christ's undying love. She had served her new Master so well and so long that she heard[1] a voice praising Him when all other voices were beyond hearing, and her response was to echo the praise.

Certainly this is an ideal, a high and noble ideal. We have called it the "Goal Supreme." We should feel no guilt when we realize how far short of it we fall. But my continuing prayer is that by the Holy Spirit I might learn to respond spontaneously to my Lord as naturally as one day I did to the devil. Is this an unrealistic and an impossible dream? I think not. May God grant that it become reality.

Thus, we close our study of the question, How can I live a holy life when I have so many human weaknesses? Is it not because a loving God sees beyond our failures to our deepest needs?

Epilogue

Soon after the crisis described in the Prologue, I attempted to put my "discovery" into a message. My preacher friend Bob, who had shared that heart-searching quest, then invited me to preach in his church specifically on this subject. I wasn't prepared for what happened! At the close of the service an elderly lady, leaning on a cane, made her way to the front. (I later learned that she was over 90 years of age.) When she reached me, she dropped her cane and literally fell into my arms. With her head on my shoulder, she wept convulsively, until my jacket was wet. When she had regained her composure, she looked into my face and spoke. Her words still ring in my ears, well over 35 years later: "Son, if I could have heard that 60 years ago, only God knows the hell I would have missed. Don't let anyone or anything ever stop you from sharing this truth."

From that day to this I have tried not to. In every church I have pastored since, the message of this book has been preached. The one sermon developed into a series. Now, in over 100 churches throughout many sections of our country, I have shared the contents of this book. Often it has been in Saturday seminars lasting about three hours. I have come to realize that this is the number one concern of those who take seriously the scriptural imperative to live a holy life. "How can I live a holy life when I have so many human weaknesses?" Always there has been the same grateful response, as searching souls have seen the distinction between the treasure and the vessel. To my knowledge, this truth has not provided them with an excuse or justification for sinful living. Instead, they have found a new peace as they daily seek more perfectly to *express outwardly* in their lives the treasure of love they have *experienced inwardly* in their hearts.

Notes

CHAPTER 1

1. For a brief discussion of positional holiness as taught in the New Testament, cf. Richard E. Howard, *Newness of Life: A Study in the Thought of Paul* (Kansas City: Beacon Hill Press of Kansas City, 1975), 96.

CHAPTER 4

1. The Greek term is *metamorphoō*. This word is always used in the Greek present tense, which depicts progression. Our modern word *metamorphosis* is a transliteration of the Greek word.

CHAPTER 5

1. For a brief but thorough treatment of Paul's theology cf. Howard, *Newness of Life*, especially Parts III and IV.
2. Cf. ibid., 37-44.

CHAPTER 6

1. For a more detailed examination of life's hurts cf. Richard E. Howard, *Where on Earth Is God?* (Kansas City: Beacon Hill Press of Kansas City, 1983), Section I.

PART III

1. Cf. Howard, *Newness of Life*, Part I.

CHAPTER 7

1. Ibid., 20.
2. Actually Paul is the only one, with a couple of minor exceptions, who used the term *nous* (mind), and then not with the typical Greek meaning. For him "heart" and "mind" are virtually synonymous, with the mind emphasizing the rational activity of the inner self. Cf. Howard, *Newness of Life*, 23-24.
3. Ibid., 20-21.
4. Ibid., 24-25.
5. Luke was the only non-Jewish writer in the Bible, and he was extensively influenced by Paul and his Semitic ideas.

CHAPTER 9

1. Cf. Howard, *Newness of Life*, chap. 4.

Chapter 12

1. A example of this is in Harold Lindsell's recent book, *The Holy Spirit in the Latter Days* (Nashville: Thomas Nelson Publishers, 1983), chap. 9. The distinguished former editor of *Christianity Today* strikingly reveals his lack of acquaintance with representative Wesleyan scholarship. He makes no reference to the abundant material by recognized scholars today who would unequivocally deny any claim to "sinless perfection." Instead, he cites the statement (one sentence!) from one very old "holiness book" (A. M. Hills, *Holiness and Power,* 1897). His argument that Wesleyans teach sinless perfection is based on Hills' statement that in sanctification one is "freed from the tendency to sin." He erroneously concludes that this assertion can only be understood as teaching sinless perfection and, beyond that, eternal security. The extent of Lindsell's deficient knowledge of Wesleyanism is embarrassingly seen in his reference to the Pilgrim Holiness denomination, which ceased to exist in 1968.

Chapter 13

1. William Barclay gives a condensed description of the basic nature of Gnosticism: "The basic doctrine of Gnosticism was that matter is essentially evil and spirit is essentially good. The Gnostics went on to argue that since that is so God Himself cannot touch matter, therefore, God did not create the world. What God did was to put out a series of emanations. Each of these emanations was further from God, until at last there was an emanation so distant from God that it could touch matter. That emanation was the creator of the world . . . Some of the Gnostics held that Jesus had no real body. A body is matter and God could not touch matter; they therefore held that Jesus was a kind of phantom without real flesh and blood" (*Daily Study Bible* [Philadelphia: Westminster Press, 1956], John 1:27-28).

Chapter 14

1. Cf. the brief discussion of the problems in the Corinthian church in Richard E. Howard, *Tongues Speaking in the New Testament,* 26-27.

2. In the first century the word *corinthianize* meant to be immoral.

Chapter 15

1. It is very significant that the Greek word most often translated "discipline" (also "chastize," "chasten," "scourge") is *paideuō*. Its first meaning is "instruct, train, educate" (Acts 7:22; 22:3). A second meaning is "correct, give guidance to" (2 Tim. 2:25; Titus 2:12). Its third meaning is "discipline with punishment" (1 Cor. 11:32; 2 Cor. 6:9). Cf. W. F. Arndt and F. W. Gingrich, *A Greek-English Lexicon of the New Testament* (Chicago: University of Chicago Press, 1957).

2. When Jesus was "transformed" (transfigured) the crisis tense (aorist) is used (Matt. 17:2; Mark 9:2).

Chapter 17

1. Matt. 4:1-11; Mark 1:12-13; Luke 4:1-13. *Peirasmos* (temptation) has the larger meaning of "to test" or "to try." Jesus' experience in the Judean wilderness was much more than simply being enticed to do evil. He was being tested and tried by Satan. But *peirasmos* can have the more limited meaning of solicitation to evil. Cf. James 1:13-14; Howard, *Newness of Life,* 195.

2. Cf. Gal. 5:17, where the desires of the flesh and Spirit are contrasted. To be sure, the verb form *(epithumeō)* is used and is not repeated a second time. But this is simply an example of the use of ellipsis, a sort of Greek shorthand. The NASB translates it "sets its desire" (both flesh and Spirit). The RSV changes the verb to a noun translation and speaks of both the desires of the flesh and Spirit. It is very misleading to give *epithumia* the intrinsic meaning of "lust." Cf. author's comments, "Galatians," *Beacon Bible Commentary* (Kansas City: Beacon Hill Press of Kansas City, 1965), 9:93 ff.

3. BBC, 9:93 ff.

Chapter 18

1. It is very significant that the Greek term for "will" *(thelēmata)* also means "desire." The two, will and desire, are vitally related. The verb form *(thelō)* means "to will" or "to wish."

2. The context makes it clear that the fear which perfect love removes is for the coming day of judgment. "By this love is perfected with us, that we may have confidence in the day of judgment; because as he is, so also are we in this world. There is no fear in love; but perfect love casts out fear, because fear involves punishment, and the one who fears is not perfected in love" (1 John 4:17-18).

Chapter 19

1. Note how Paul specifically described the desire *(epithumian)* as evil *(kakēn).*

2. As noted in chap. 17, the word "temptation" *(peirasmos)* means far more than our modern concept of "enticement to evil," as it did in 17th-century England (when the KJV was translated). Its basic meaning is "to test" or "to try," which includes the modern idea. This verse certainly applies to temptation through our desires.

3. Cf. Howard, *Where on Earth Is God?* chap. 27.

4. The illustration of smoking is used only because it presents a struggle easily understood.

CHAPTER 20

1. Cf. the sex education program of a Protestant denomination that included explicit pictures and tape recordings of adults engaged in varied sexual activity, including such abnormalities as homosexuality and masturbation, reported in a prominent national news magazine. Later the church was prosecuted for pornography by the state of Wisconsin.

2. Cf. Mark 3:5. When the NT speaks of God's (or Jesus') anger, the word is usually *orgē*. The other word for anger *(thumos)* is only used of God in a few remote places, generally with orgē (cf. Rom. 2:8 and Revelation). The word used in the works of the flesh (Gal. 5:20, obviously evil) is *thumos*.

CHAPTER 21

1. William Barclay repeatedly emphasized this in his NT commentary, *The Daily Study Bible.*

2. Cf. Arndt and Gingrich, *A Greek-English Lexicon.*

3. E.g., "a people for His own possession, zealous for good deeds" (NASB).

CHAPTER 22

1. As noted in chap. 8, we are arbitrarily using *personhood* for the inner self and *personality* for the outer self.

CHAPTER 23

1. Cf. chap. 20, n. 2.

CHAPTER 24

1. Marvin R. Vincent, *Word Studies in the New Testament,* vol. 3 (New York: Charles Scribner's Sons, 1889).

CHAPTER 26

1. It is most unfortunate that a vast majority of times this verse is stripped of much of its meaning when a second "able" is added: "[God] is able to do . . . beyond all that we *are able to* ask or think." That italized addition is not in the scripture! Of course God is able to do more than we are *able* to ask or think. But the promise is God's ability to do more than we *do* ask or think.

2. The Greek term for "works" is *energeō,* which we transliterate as *energize* and *energy* (noun).

3. Cf. Phil. 2:12-13, where Paul speaks about our work *(katergazomi)* and God's work *(energeō).*

4. A. W. Tozer, *That Incredible Christian* (Harrisburg, Pa.: Christian Publications, 1964), 54-55.

CHAPTER 27

1. It is quite generally thought that hearing is the last of our senses to be lost.